Consumer Credit Ac

CHAPTER 39

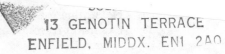

13 GENOTIN TERRACE
ENFIELD, MIDDX. EN1 2AO

ARRANGEMENT OF SECTIONS

A

PART V

ENTRY INTO CREDIT OR HIRE AGREEMENTS

Preliminary matters

Making the agreement

Cancellation of certain agreements within cooling-off period

Exclusion of certain agreements from Part V

PART VI

MATTERS ARISING DURING CURRENCY OF CREDIT OR HIRE AGREEMENTS

A 2

PART IX

JUDICIAL CONTROL

Enforcement of certain regulated agreements and securities

Extension of time

Protection of property pending proceedings

PART X

ANCILLARY CREDIT BUSINESSES

Definitions

ELIZABETH II

Consumer Credit Act 1974

1974 CHAPTER 39

An Act to establish for the protection of consumers a new system, administered by the Director General of Fair Trading, of licensing and other control of traders concerned with the provision of credit, or the supply of goods on hire or hire-purchase, and their transactions, in place of the present enactments regulating moneylenders, pawnbrokers and hire-purchase traders and their transactions; and for related matters.

[31st July 1974]

BE IT ENACTED by the Queen's most Excellent Majesty, by and with the advice and consent of the Lords Spiritual and Temporal, and Commons, in this present Parliament assembled, and by the authority of the same, as follows:—

PART I

DIRECTOR GENERAL OF FAIR TRADING

1.—(1) It is the duty of the Director General of Fair Trading ("the Director")—

General functions of Director

    (*a*) to administer the licensing system set up by this Act,

    (*b*) to exercise the adjudicating functions conferred on him by this Act in relation to the issue, renewal, variation, suspension and revocation of licences, and other matters,

    (*c*) generally to superintend the working and enforcement of this Act, and regulations made under it, and

    (*d*) where necessary or expedient, himself to take steps to enforce this Act, and regulations so made.

(2) It is the duty of the Director, so far as appears to him to be practicable and having regard both to the national interest and the interests of persons carrying on businesses to which this Act applies and their customers, to keep under review and from time to time advise the Secretary of State about—

> (a) social and commercial developments in the United Kingdom and elsewhere relating to the provision of credit or bailment or (in Scotland) hiring of goods to individuals, and related activities ; and

> (b) the working and enforcement of this Act and orders and regulations made under it.

2.—(1) The Secretary of State may by order—

> (a) confer on the Director additional functions concerning the provision of credit or bailment or (in Scotland) hiring of goods to individuals, and related activities, and

> (b) regulate the carrying out by the Director of his functions under this Act.

(2) The Secretary of State may give general directions indicating considerations to which the Director should have particular regard in carrying out his functions under this Act, and may give specific directions on any matter connected with the carrying out by the Director of those functions.

(3) The Secretary of State, on giving any directions under subsection (2), shall arrange for them to be published in such manner as he thinks most suitable for drawing them to the attention of interested persons.

(4) With the approval of the Secretary of State and the Treasury, the Director may charge, for any service or facility provided by him under this Act, a fee of an amount specified by general notice (the " specified fee ").

(5) Provision may be made under subsection (4) for reduced fees, or no fees at all, to be paid for certain services or facilities by persons of a specified description, and references in this Act to the specified fee shall, in such cases, be construed accordingly.

(6) An order under subsection (1)(a) shall be made by statutory instrument and shall be of no effect unless a draft of the order has been laid before and approved by each House of Parliament.

(7) References in subsection (2) to the functions of the Director under this Act do not include the making of a determination to which section 41 or 150 (appeals from Director to Secretary of State) applies.

3. The Tribunals and Inquiries Act 1971 is amended as follows (the amendments bringing the adjudicating functions of the Director under this Act under the supervision of the Council on Tribunals)—

PART I
THE
DIRECTOR
Supervision
by Council
on Tribunals.
1971 c. 62.

> (*a*) in section 8(2), insert " 5A " after " paragraph " ;
>
> (*b*) in section 19(4), insert " or the Director General of Fair Trading referred to in paragraph 5A " after " or 46 " ;
>
> (*c*) in Schedule 1, after paragraph 5, insert—

" Consumer credit

> 5A. The Director General of Fair Trading, in respect of his functions under the Consumer Credit Act 1974 (c. 39), and any member of the Director's staff authorised to exercise those functions under paragraph 7 of Schedule 1 to the Fair Trading Act 1973."

4. The Director shall arrange for the dissemination, in such form and manner as he considers appropriate, of such information and advice as it may appear to him expedient to give to the public in the United Kingdom about the operation of this Act, the credit facilities available to them, and other matters within the scope of his functions under this Act.

5. At the end of subsection (2) of section 125 (annual and other reports of Director) of the Fair Trading Act 1973 insert " and shall set out any directions given to the Director under section 2(2) of the Consumer Credit Act 1974 during that year ".

6.—(1) An application to the Director under this Act is of no effect unless the requirements of this section are satisfied.

(2) The application must be in writing, and in such form, and accompanied by such particulars, as the Director may specify by general notice, and must be accompanied by the specified fee.

(3) After giving preliminary consideration to an application, the Director may by notice require the applicant to furnish him with such further information relevant to the application as may be described in the notice, and may require any information furnished by the applicant (whether at the time of the application or subsequently) to be verified in such manner as the Director may stipulate.

(4) The Director may by notice require the applicant to publish details of his application at a time or times and in a manner specified in the notice.

Penalty
for false
information.

7. A person who, in connection with any application or request to the Director under this Act, or in response to any invitation or requirement of the Director under this Act, knowingly or recklessly gives information to the Director which, in a material particular, is false or misleading, commits an offence.

PART II

CREDIT AGREEMENTS, HIRE AGREEMENTS AND LINKED TRANSACTIONS

Consumer
credit
agreements.

8.—(1) A personal credit agreement is an agreement between an individual (" the debtor ") and any other person (" the creditor ") by which the creditor provides the debtor with credit of any amount.

(2) A consumer credit agreement is a personal credit agreement by which the creditor provides the debtor with credit not exceeding £5,000.

(3) A consumer credit agreement is a regulated agreement within the meaning of this Act if it is not an agreement (an " exempt agreement ") specified in or under section 16.

Meaning
of credit.

9.—(1) In this Act " credit " includes a cash loan, and any other form of financial accommodation.

(2) Where credit is provided otherwise than in sterling it shall be treated for the purposes of this Act as provided in sterling of an equivalent amount.

(3) Without prejudice to the generality of subsection (1), the person by whom goods are bailed or (in Scotland) hired to an individual under a hire-purchase agreement shall be taken to provide him with fixed-sum credit to finance the transaction of an amount equal to the total price of the goods less the aggregate of the deposit (if any) and the total charge for credit.

(4) For the purposes of this Act, an item entering into the total charge for credit shall not be treated as credit even though time is allowed for its payment.

Running-
account
credit and
fixed-sum
credit.

10.—(1) For the purposes of this Act—

    (*a*) running-account credit is a facility under a personal credit agreement whereby the debtor is enabled to receive from time to time (whether in his own person, or by another person) from the creditor or a third party cash, goods and services (or any of them) to an amount or value such that, taking into account payments made by or to the credit of the debtor, the credit limit (if any) is not at any time exceeded ; and

(b) fixed-sum credit is any other facility under a personal credit agreement whereby the debtor is enabled to receive credit (whether in one amount or by instalments).

(2) In relation to running-account credit, " credit limit " means, as respects any period, the maximum debit balance which, under the credit agreement, is allowed to stand on the account during that period, disregarding any term of the agreement allowing that maximum to be exceeded merely temporarily.

(3) For the purposes of section 8(2), running-account credit shall be taken not to exceed the amount specified in that subsection (" the specified amount ") if—

(a) the credit limit does not exceed the specified amount ; or

(b) whether or not there is a credit limit, and if there is, notwithstanding that it exceeds the specified amount,—

(i) the debtor is not enabled to draw at any one time an amount which, so far as (having regard to section 9(4)) it represents credit, exceeds the specified amount, or

(ii) the agreement provides that, if the debit balance rises above a given amount (not exceeding the specified amount), the rate of the total charge for credit increases or any other condition favouring the creditor or his associate comes into operation, or

(iii) at the time the agreement is made it is probable, having regard to the terms of the agreement and any other relevant considerations, that the debit balance will not at any time rise above the specified amount.

11.—(1) A restricted-use credit agreement is a regulated consumer credit agreement—

Restricted-use credit and unrestricted-use credit.

(a) to finance a transaction between the debtor and the creditor, whether forming part of that agreement or not, or

(b) to finance a transaction between the debtor and a person (the " supplier ") other than the creditor, or

(c) to refinance any existing indebtedness of the debtor's, whether to the creditor or another person,

and " restricted-use credit " shall be construed accordingly.

(2) An unrestricted-use credit agreement is a regulated consumer credit agreement not falling within subsection (1), and " unrestricted-use credit " shall be construed accordingly.

(3) An agreement does not fall within subsection (1) if the credit is in fact provided in such a way as to leave the debtor free to use it as he chooses, even though certain uses would contravene that or any other agreement.

(4) An agreement may fall within subsection (1)(*b*) although the identity of the supplier is unknown at the time the agreement is made.

Debtor-
creditor
supplier
agreements.
12. A debtor-creditor-supplier agreement is a regulated consumer credit agreement being—

   (*a*) a restricted-use credit agreement which falls within section 11(1)(*a*), or

   (*b*) a restricted-use credit agreement which falls within section 11(1)(*b*) and is made by the creditor under pre-existing arrangements, or in contemplation of future arrangements, between himself and the supplier, or

   (*c*) an unrestricted-use credit agreement which is made by the creditor under pre-existing arrangements between himself and a person (the " supplier ") other than the debtor in the knowledge that the credit is to be used to finance a transaction between the debtor and the supplier.

Debtor-
creditor
agreements.
13. A debtor-creditor agreement is a regulated consumer credit agreement being—

   (*a*) a restricted-use credit agreement which falls within section 11(1)(*b*) but is not made by the creditor under pre-existing arrangements, or in contemplation of future arrangements, between himself and the supplier, or

   (*b*) a restricted-use credit agreement which falls within section 11(1)(*c*), or

   (*c*) an unrestricted-use credit agreement which is not made by the creditor under pre-existing arrangements between himself and a person (the " supplier ") other than the debtor in the knowledge that the credit is to be used to finance a transaction between the debtor and the supplier.

Credit-token
agreements.
14.—(1) A credit-token is a card, check, voucher, coupon, stamp, form, booklet or other document or thing given to an individual by a person carrying on a consumer credit business, who undertakes—

   (*a*) that on the production of it (whether or not some other action is also required) he will supply cash, goods and services (or any of them) on credit, or

(b) that where, on the production of it to a third party (whether or not any other action is also required), the third party supplies cash, goods and services (or any of them), he will pay the third party for them (whether or not deducting any discount or commission), in return for payment to him by the individual.

PART II
CREDIT
AGREE-
MENTS ETC.

(2) A credit-token agreement is a regulated agreement for the provision of credit in connection with the use of a credit-token.

(3) Without prejudice to the generality of section 9(1), the person who gives to an individual an undertaking falling within subsection (1)(b) shall be taken to provide him with credit drawn on whenever a third party supplies him with cash, goods or services.

(4) For the purposes of subsection (1), use of an object to operate a machine provided by the person giving the object or a third party shall be treated as the production of the object to him.

15.—(1) A consumer hire agreement is an agreement made by a person with an individual (the " hirer ") for the bailment or (in Scotland) the hiring of goods to the hirer, being an agreement which—

Consumer
hire
agreements.

(a) is not a hire-purchase agreement, and

(b) is capable of subsisting for more than three months, and

(c) does not require the hirer to make payments exceeding £5,000.

(2) A consumer hire agreement is a regulated agreement if it is not an exempt agreement.

16.—(1) This Act does not regulate a consumer credit agreement where the creditor is a local authority or building society, or a body specified, or of a description specified, in an order made by the Secretary of State, being—

Exempt
agreements.

(a) an insurance company,

(b) a friendly society,

(c) an organisation of employers or organisation of workers,

(d) a charity,

(e) a land improvement company, or

(f) a body corporate named or specifically referred to in any public general Act.

(2) Subsection (1) applies only where the agreement is—

(a) a debtor-creditor-supplier agreement financing—

(i) the purchase of land, or

(ii) the provision of dwellings on any land,

and secured by a land mortgage on that land ; or

(b) a debtor-creditor agreement secured by any land mortgage ; or

(c) a debtor-creditor-supplier agreement financing a transaction which is a linked transaction in relation to—

(i) an agreement falling within paragraph (a), or

(ii) an agreement falling within paragraph (b) financing—

(aa) the purchase of any land, or

(bb) the provision of dwellings on any land,

and secured by a land mortgage on the land referred to in paragraph (a) or, as the case may be, the land referred to in sub-paragraph (ii).

(3) The Secretary of State shall not make, vary or revoke an order—

(a) under subsection (1)(a) without consulting the Minister of the Crown responsible for insurance companies,

(b) under subsection (1)(b) or (c) without consulting the Chief Registrar of Friendly Societies,

(c) under subsection (1)(d) without consulting the Charity Commissioners, or

(d) under subsection (1)(e) or (f) without consulting any Minister of the Crown with responsibilities concerning the body in question.

(4) An order under subsection (1) relating to a body may be limited so as to apply only to agreements by that body of a description specified in the order.

(5) The Secretary of State may by order provide that this Act shall not regulate other consumer credit agreements where—

(a) the number of payments to be made by the debtor does not exceed the number specified for that purpose in the order, or

(b) the rate of the total charge for credit does not exceed the rate so specified, or

(c) an agreement has a connection with a country outside the United Kingdom.

(6) The Secretary of State may by order provide that this Act shall not regulate consumer hire agreements of a description specified in the order where—

(a) the owner is a body corporate authorised by or under any enactment to supply electricity, gas or water, and

(b) the subject of the agreement is a meter or metering equipment,

or where the owner is the Post Office or the Kingston upon Hull City Council.

(7) Nothing in this section affects the application of sections 137 to 140 (extortionate credit bargains).

(8) In the application of this section to Scotland subsection (3)(c) shall not have effect.

(9) In the application of this section to Northern Ireland subsection (3) shall have effect as if any reference to a Minister of the Crown were a reference to a Northern Ireland department, any reference to the Chief Registrar of Friendly Societies were a reference to the Registrar of Friendly Societies for Northern Ireland, and any reference to the Charity Commissioners were a reference to the Department of Finance for Northern Ireland.

17.—(1) A small agreement is—

(a) a regulated consumer credit agreement for credit not exceeding £30, other than a hire-purchase or conditional sale agreement ; or

(b) a regulated consumer hire agreement which does not require the hirer to make payments exceeding £30,

being an agreement which is either unsecured or secured by a guarantee or indemnity only (whether or not the guarantee or indemnity is itself secured).

(2) Section 10(3)(a) applies for the purposes of subsection (1) as it applies for the purposes of section 8(2).

(3) Where—

(a) two or more small agreements are made at or about the same time between the same parties, and

(b) it appears probable that they would instead have been made as a single agreement but for the desire to avoid the operation of provisions of this Act which would have applied to that single agreement but, apart from this subsection, are not applicable to the small agreements,

this Act applies to the small agreements as if they were regulated agreements other than small agreements.

(4) If, apart from this subsection, subsection (3) does not apply to any agreements but would apply if, for any party or parties to any of the agreements, there were substituted an associate of that party, or associates of each of those parties, as the case may be, then subsection (3) shall apply to the agreements.

PART II
CREDIT
AGREE-
MENTS ETC.

Small
agreements.

PART II
CREDIT
AGREE-
MENTS ETC.
Multiple
agreements.

18.—(1) This section applies to an agreement (a "multiple agreement") if its terms are such as—

(*a*) to place a part of it within one category of agreement mentioned in this Act, and another part of it within a different category of agreement so mentioned, or within a category of agreement not so mentioned, or

(*b*) to place it, or a part of it, within two or more categories of agreement so mentioned.

(2) Where a part of an agreement falls within subsection (1), that part shall be treated for the purposes of this Act as a separate agreement.

(3) Where an agreement falls within subsection (1)(*b*), it shall be treated as an agreement in each of the categories in question, and this Act shall apply to it accordingly.

(4) Where under subsection (2) a part of a multiple agreement is to be treated as a separate agreement, the multiple agreement shall (with any necessary modifications) be construed accordingly; and any sum payable under the multiple agreement, if not apportioned by the parties, shall for the purposes of proceedings in any court relating to the multiple agreement be apportioned by the court as may be requisite.

(5) In the case of an agreement for running-account credit, a term of the agreement allowing the credit limit to be exceeded merely temporarily shall not be treated as a separate agreement or as providing fixed-sum credit in respect of the excess.

(6) This Act does not apply to a multiple agreement so far as the agreement relates to goods if under the agreement payments are to be made in respect of the goods in the form of rent (other than a rentcharge) issuing out of land.

19.—(1) A transaction entered into by the debtor or hirer, or a relative of his, with any other person ("the other party"), except one for the provision of security, is a linked transaction in relation to an actual or prospective regulated agreement (the "principal agreement") of which it does not form part if—

(*a*) the transaction is entered into in compliance with a term of the principal agreement; or

(*b*) the principal agreement is a debtor-creditor-supplier agreement and the transaction is financed, or to be financed, by the principal agreement; or

(*c*) the other party is a person mentioned in subsection (2), and a person so mentioned initiated the transaction by suggesting it to the debtor or hirer, or his relative, who enters into it—

(i) to induce the creditor or owner to enter into the principal agreement, or

(ii) for another purpose related to the principal agreement, or

(iii) where the principal agreement is a restricted-use credit agreement, for a purpose related to a transaction financed, or to be financed, by the principal agreement.

(2) The persons referred to in subsection (1)(c) are—

(a) the creditor or owner, or his associate ;

(b) a person who, in the negotiation of the transaction, is represented by a credit-broker who is also a negotiator in antecedent negotiations for the principal agreement ;

(c) a person who, at the time the transaction is initiated, knows that the principal agreement has been made or contemplates that it might be made.

(3) A linked transaction entered into before the making of the principal agreement has no effect until such time (if any) as that agreement is made.

(4) Regulations may exclude linked transactions of the pre-scribed description from the operation of subsection (3).

20.—(1) The Secretary of State shall make regulations con-taining such provisions as appear to him appropriate for determining the true cost to the debtor of the credit provided or to be provided under an actual or prospective consumer credit agreement (the " total charge for credit "), and regulations so made shall prescribe— *Total charge for credit.*

(a) what items are to be treated as entering into the total charge for credit, and how their amount is to be ascer-tained ;

(b) the method of calculating the rate of the total charge for credit.

(2) Regulations under subsection (1) may provide for the whole or part of the amount payable by the debtor or his relative under any linked transaction to be included in the total charge for credit, whether or not the creditor is a party to the transaction or derives benefit from it.

Part III

Licensing of Credit and Hire Businesses

Licensing principles

21.—(1) Subject to this section, a licence is required to carry on a consumer credit business or consumer hire business.

(2) A local authority does not need a licence to carry on a business.

(3) A body corporate empowered by a public general Act naming it to carry on a business does not need a licence to do so.

22.—(1) A licence may be—

(a) a standard licence, that is a licence, issued by the Director to a person named in the licence on an application made by him, which, during the prescribed period, covers such activities as are described in the licence, or

(b) a group licence, that is a licence, issued by the Director (whether on the application of any person or of his own motion), which, during such period as the Director thinks fit or, if he thinks fit, indefinitely, covers such persons and activities as are described in the licence.

(2) A licence is not assignable or, subject to section 37, transmissible on death or in any other way.

(3) Except in the case of a partnership or an unincorporated body of persons, a standard licence shall not be issued to more than one person.

(4) A standard licence issued to a partnership or an unincorporated body of persons shall be issued in the name of the partnership or body.

(5) The Director may issue a group licence only if it appears to him that the public interest is better served by doing so than by obliging the persons concerned to apply separately for standard licences.

(6) The persons covered by a group licence may be described by general words, whether or not coupled with the exclusion of named persons, or in any other way the Director thinks fit.

(7) The fact that a person is covered by a group licence in respect of certain activities does not prevent a standard licence being issued to him in respect of those activities or any of them.

(8) A group licence issued on the application of any person shall be issued to that person, and general notice shall be given of the issue of any group licence (whether on application or not).

23.—(1) Subject to this section, a licence to carry on a business covers all lawful activities done in the course of that business, whether by the licensee or other persons on his behalf.

(2) A licence may limit the activities it covers, whether by authorising the licensee to enter into certain types of agreement only, or in any other way.

(3) A licence covers the canvassing off trade premises of debtor-creditor-supplier agreements or regulated consumer hire agreements only if, and to the extent that, the licence-specifically so provides ; and such provision shall not be included in a group licence.

(4) Regulations may be made specifying other activities which, if engaged in by or on behalf of the person carrying on a business, require to be covered by an express term in his licence.

24. A standard licence authorises the licensee to carry on a business under the name or names specified in the licence, but not under any other name.

25.—(1) A standard licence shall be granted on the application of any person if he satisfies the Director that—

    (*a*) he is a fit person to engage in activities covered by the licence, and

    (*b*) the name or names under which he applies to be licensed is or are not misleading or otherwise undesirable.

(2) In determining whether an applicant for a standard licence is a fit person to engage in any activities, the Director shall have regard to any circumstances appearing to him to be relevant, and in particular any evidence tending to show that the applicant, or any of the applicant's employees, agents or associates (whether past or present) or, where the applicant is a body corporate, any person appearing to the Director to be a controller of the body corporate or an associate of any such person, has—

    (*a*) committed any offence involving fraud or other dishonesty, or violence,

    (*b*) contravened any provision made by or under this Act, or by or under any other enactment regulating the provision of credit to individuals or other transactions with individuals,

(c) practised discrimination on grounds of sex, colour, race or ethnic or national origins in, or in connection with, the carrying on of any business, or

(d) engaged in business practices appearing to the Director to be deceitful or oppressive, or otherwise unfair or improper (whether unlawful or not).

(3) In subsection (2), " associate ", in addition to the persons specified in section 184, includes a business associate.

Conduct of business.

26. Regulations may be made as to the conduct by a licensee of his business, and may in particular specify—

(a) the books and other records to be kept by him, and

(b) the information to be furnished by him to persons with whom he does business or seeks to do business, and the way it is to be furnished.

Issue of licences

Determination of applications.

27.—(1) Unless the Director determines to issue a licence in accordance with an application he shall, before determining the application, by notice—

(a) inform the applicant, giving his reasons, that, as the case may be, he is minded to refuse the application, or to grant it in terms different from those applied for, describing them, and

(b) invite the applicant to submit to the Director representations in support of his application in accordance with section 34.

(2) If the Director grants the application in terms different from those applied for then, whether or not the applicant appeals, the Director shall issue the licence in the terms approved by him unless the applicant by notice informs him that he does not desire a licence in those terms.

Exclusion from group licence.

28. Where the Director is minded to issue a group licence (whether on the application of any person or not), and in doing so to exclude any person from the group by name, he shall, before determining the matter,—

(a) give notice of that fact to the person proposed to be excluded, giving his reasons, and

(b) invite that person to submit to the Director representations against his exclusion in accordance with section 34.

Renewal, variation, suspension and revocation of licences

29.—(1) If the licensee under a standard licence, or the original applicant for, or any licensee under, a group licence of limited duration, wishes the Director to renew the licence, whether on the same terms (except as to expiry) or on varied terms, he must, during the period specified by the Director by general notice or such longer period as the Director may allow, make an application to the Director for its renewal.

(2) The Director may of his own motion renew any group licence.

(3) The preceding provisions of this Part apply to the renewal of a licence as they apply to the issue of a licence, except that section 28 does not apply to a person who was already excluded in the licence up for renewal.

(4) Until the determination of an application under subsection (1) and, where an appeal lies from the determination, until the end of the appeal period, the licence shall continue in force, notwithstanding that apart from this subsection it would expire earlier.

(5) On the refusal of an application under this section, the Director may give directions authorising a licensee to carry into effect agreements made by him before the expiry of the licence.

(6) General notice shall be given of the renewal of a group licence.

30.—(1) On an application made by the licensee, the Director Variation may if he thinks fit by notice to the licensee vary a standard by request. licence in accordance with the application.

(2) In the case of a group licence issued on the application of any person, the Director, on an application made by that person, may if he thinks fit by notice to that person vary the terms of the licence in accordance with the application ; but the Director shall not vary a group licence under this subsection by excluding a named person, other than the person making the request, unless that named person consents in writing to his exclusion.

(3) In the case of a group licence from which (whether by name or description) a person is excluded, the Director, on an application made by that person, may if he thinks fit, by notice to that person, vary the terms of the licence so as to remove the exclusion.

(4) Unless the Director determines to vary a licence in accordance with an application he shall, before determining the application, by notice—

    (a) inform the applicant, giving his reasons, that he is minded to refuse the application, and

    (b) invite the applicant to submit to the Director representations in support of his application in accordance with section 34.

(5) General notice shall be given that a variation of a group licence has been made under this section.

31.—(1) Where at a time during the currency of a licence the Director is of the opinion that, if the licence had expired at that time, he would, on an application for its renewal or further renewal on the same terms (except as to expiry), have been minded to grant the application but on different terms, and that therefore the licence should be varied, he shall proceed as follows.

(2) In the case of a standard licence the Director shall, by notice—

    (a) inform the licensee of the variations the Director is minded to make in the terms of the licence, stating his reasons, and

    (b) invite him to submit to the Director representations as to the proposed variations in accordance with section 34.

(3) In the case of a group licence the Director shall—

    (a) give general notice of the variations he is minded to make in the terms of the licence, stating his reasons, and

    (b) in the notice invite any licensee to submit to him representations as to the proposed variations in accordance with section 34.

(4) In the case of a group licence issued on application the Director shall also—

    (a) inform the original applicant of the variations the Director is minded to make in the terms of the licence, stating his reasons, and

    (b) invite him to submit to the Director representations as to the proposed variations in accordance with section 34.

(5) If the Director is minded to vary a group licence by excluding any person (other than the original applicant) from the group by name the Director shall, in addition, take the like steps under section 28 as are required in the case mentioned in that section.

(6) General notice shall be given that a variation of any group licence has been made under this section.

(7) A variation under this section shall not take effect before the end of the appeal period.

32.—(1) Where at a time during the currency of a licence the Director is of the opinion that if the licence had expired at that time he would have been minded not to renew it, and that therefore it should be revoked or suspended, he shall proceed as follows.

(2) In the case of a standard licence the Director shall, by notice—

    (*a*) inform the licensee that, as the case may be, the Director is minded to revoke the licence, or suspend it until a specified date or indefinitely, stating his reasons, and

    (*b*) invite him to submit representations as to the proposed revocation or suspension in accordance with section 34.

(3) In the case of a group licence the Director shall—

    (*a*) give general notice that, as the case may be, he is minded to revoke the licence, or suspend it until a specified date or indefinitely, stating his reasons, and

    (*b*) in the notice invite any licensee to submit to him representations as to the proposed revocation or suspension in accordance with section 34.

(4) In the case of a group licence issued on application the Director shall also—

    (*a*) inform the original applicant that, as the case may be, the Director is minded to revoke the licence, or suspend it until a specified date or indefinitely, stating his reasons, and

    (*b*) invite him to submit representations as to the proposed revocation or suspension in accordance with section 34.

(5) If he revokes or suspends the licence, the Director may give directions authorising a licensee to carry into effect agreements made by him before the revocation or suspension.

(6) General notice shall be given of the revocation or suspension of a group licence.

(7) A revocation or suspension under this section shall not take effect before the end of the appeal period.

(8) Except for the purposes of section 29, a licensee under a suspended licence shall be treated, in respect of the period of suspension, as if the licence had not been issued ; and where

the suspension is not expressed to end on a specified date it may, if the Director thinks fit, be ended by notice given by him to the licensee or, in the case of a group licence, by general notice.

Application
to end
suspension.
33.—(1) On an application made by a licensee the Director may, if he thinks fit, by notice to the licensee end the suspension of a licence, whether the suspension was for a fixed or indefinite period.

(2) Unless the Director determines to end the suspension in accordance with the application he shall, before determining the application, by notice—

(a) inform the applicant, giving his reasons, that he is minded to refuse the application, and

(b) invite the applicant to submit to the Director representations in support of his application in accordance with section 34.

(3) General notice shall be given that a suspension of a group licence has been ended under this section.

(4) In the case of a group licence issued on application—

(a) the references in subsection (1) to a licensee include the original applicant;

(b) the Director shall inform the original applicant that a suspension of a group licence has been ended under this section.

Miscellaneous

Representa-
tions to
Director.
34.—(1) Where this section applies to an invitation by the Director to any person to submit representations, the Director shall invite that person, within 21 days after the notice containing the invitation is given to him or published, or such longer period as the Director may allow,—

(a) to submit his representations in writing to the Director, and

(b) to give notice to the Director, if he thinks fit, that he wishes to make representations orally,

and where notice is given under paragraph (b) the Director shall arrange for the oral representations to be heard.

(2) In reaching his determination the Director shall take into account any representations submitted or made under this section.

(3) The Director shall give notice of his determination to the persons who were required to be invited to submit representations about it or, where the invitation to submit representations was required to be given by general notice, shall give general notice of the determination.

35.—(1) The Director shall establish and maintain a register, in which he shall cause to be kept particulars of—

> (*a*) applications not yet determined for the issue, variation or renewal of licences, or for ending the suspension of a licence;
>
> (*b*) licences which are in force, or have at any time been suspended or revoked, with details of any variation of the terms of a licence;
>
> (*c*) decisions given by him under this Act, and any appeal from those decisions ; and
>
> (*d*) such other matters (if any) as he thinks fit.

(2) The Director shall give general notice of the various matters required to be entered in the register, and of any change in them made under subsection (1)(*d*).

(3) Any person shall be entitled on payment of the specified fee—

> (*a*) to inspect the register during ordinary office hours and take copies of any entry, or
>
> (*b*) to obtain from the Director a copy, certified by the Director to be correct, of any entry in the register.

(4) The Director may, if he thinks fit, determine that the right conferred by subsection (3)(*a*) shall be exercisable in relation to a copy of the register instead of, or in addition to, the original.

(5) The Director shall give general notice of the place or places where, and times when, the register or a copy of it may be inspected.

36.—(1) Within 21 working days after a change takes place in any particulars entered in the register in respect of a standard licence or the licensee under section 35(1)(*d*) (not being a change resulting from action taken by the Director), the licensee shall give the Director notice of the change; and the Director shall cause any necessary amendment to be made in the register.

(2) Within 21 working days after—

> (*a*) any change takes place in the officers of—
>
>> (i) a body corporate, or an unincorporated body of persons, which is the licensee under a standard licence, or
>>
>> (ii) a body corporate which is a controller of a body corporate which is such a licensee, or
>
> (*b*) a body corporate which is such a licensee becomes aware that a person has become or ceased to be a controller of the body corporate, or

(c) any change takes place in the members of a partnership which is such a licensee (including a change on the amalgamation of the partnership with another firm, or a change whereby the number of partners is reduced to one),

the licensee shall give the Director notice of the change.

(3) Within 14 working days after any change takes place in the officers of a body corporate which is a controller of another body corporate which is a licensee under a standard licence, the controller shall give the licensee notice of the change.

(4) Within 14 working days after a person becomes or ceases to be a controller of a body corporate which is a licensee under a standard licence, that person shall give the licensee notice of the fact.

(5) Where a change in a partnership has the result that the business ceases to be carried on under the name, or any of the names, specified in a standard licence the licence shall cease to have effect.

(6) Where the Director is given notice under sub-section (1) or (2) of any change, and subsection (5) does not apply, the Director may by notice require the licensee to furnish him with such information, verified in such manner, as the Director may stipulate.

Death,
bankruptcy
etc. of
licensee.

37.—(1) A licence held by one individual terminates if he—

(a) dies, or

(b) is adjudged bankrupt, or

1959 c. 22.

(c) becomes a patient within the meaning of Part VIII of the Mental Health Act 1959.

(2) In relation to a licence held by one individual, or a partnership or other unincorporated body of persons, or a body corporate, regulations may specify other events relating to the licensee on the occurrence of which the licence is to terminate.

(3) Regulations may—

(a) provide for the termination of a licence by subsection (1), or under subsection (2), to be deferred for a period not exceeding 12 months, and

(b) authorise the business of the licensee to be carried on under the licence by some other person during the period of deferment, subject to such conditions as may be prescribed.

(4) This section does not apply to group licences.

38.—(1) In the application of section 37 to Scotland the following shall be substituted for paragraphs (*b*) and (*c*) of subsection (1)—

" (*b*) has his estate sequestrated, or

    (*c*) becomes incapable of managing his own affairs."

(2) In the application of section 37 to Northern Ireland the following shall be substituted for subsection (1)—

" (1) A licence held by one individual terminates if—

    (*a*) he dies, or

    (*b*) he is adjudged bankrupt or his estate and effects vest in the official assignee under section 349 of the Irish Bankrupt and Insolvent Act 1857, or

    (*c*) a declaration is made under section 15 of the Lunacy Regulation (Ireland) Act 1871 that he is of unsound mind and incapable of managing his person or property, or an order is made under section 68 of that Act in consequence of its being found that he is of unsound mind and incapable of managing his affairs.".

39.—(1) A person who engages in any activities for which a licence is required when he is not a licensee under a licence covering those activities commits an offence.

(2) A licensee under a standard licence who carries on business under a name not specified in the licence commits an offence.

(3) A person who fails to give the Director or a licensee notice under section 36 within the period required commits an offence.

40.—(1) A regulated agreement, other than a non-commercial agreement, if made when the creditor or owner was unlicensed, is enforceable against the debtor or hirer only where the Director has made an order under this section which applies to the agreement.

(2) Where during any period an unlicensed person (the " trader ") was carrying on a consumer credit business or consumer hire business, he or his successor in title may apply to the Director for an order that regulated agreements made by the trader during that period are to be treated as if he had been licensed.

(3) Unless the Director determines to make an order under subsection (2) in accordance with the application, he shall, before determining the application, by notice—

    (*a*) inform the applicant, giving his reasons, that, as the case may be, he is minded to refuse the application, or to grant it in terms different from those applied for, describing them, and

(*b*) invite the applicant to submit to the Director representations in support of his application in accordance with section 34.

(4) In determining whether or not to make an order under subsection (2) in respect of any period the Director shall consider, in addition to any other relevant factors—

(*a*) how far, if at all, debtors or hirers under regulated agreements made by the trader during that period were prejudiced by the trader's conduct,

(*b*) whether or not the Director would have been likely to grant a licence covering that period on an application by the trader, and

(*c*) the degree of culpability for the failure to obtain a licence.

(5) If the Director thinks fit, he may in an order under subsection (2)—

(*a*) limit the order to specified agreements, or agreements of a specified description or made at a specified time ;

(*b*) make the order conditional on the doing of specified acts by the applicant.

Appeals to
Secretary of
State under
Part III.

41.—(1) If, in the case of a determination by the Director such as is mentioned in column 1 of the table set out at the end of this section, a person mentioned in relation to that determination in column 2 of the table is aggrieved by the determination he may, within the prescribed period, and in the prescribed manner, appeal to the Secretary of State.

(2) Regulations may make provision as to the persons by whom (on behalf of the Secretary of State) appeals under this section are to be heard, the manner in which they are to be conducted, and any other matter connected with such appeals.

(3) On an appeal under this section, the Secretary of State may give such directions for disposing of the appeal as he thinks just, including a direction for the payment of costs by any party to the appeal.

(4) A direction under subsection (3) for payment of costs may be made a rule of the High Court on the application of the party in whose favour it is given.

(5) In Scotland a direction under subsection (3) for payment of expenses may be enforced in like manner as a recorded decree arbitral.

TABLE

Determination	*Appellant*
Refusal to issue, renew or vary licence in accordance with terms of application.	The applicant.
Exclusion of person from group licence.	The person excluded.
Refusal to give directions in respect of a licensee under section 29(5) or 32(5).	The licensee.
Compulsory variation, or suspension or revocation, of standard licence.	The licensee.
Compulsory variation, or suspension or revocation, of group licence.	The original applicant or any licensee.
Refusal to end suspension of licence in accordance with terms of application.	The applicant.
Refusal to make order under section 40(2) in accordance with terms of application.	The applicant.

42.—(1) In section 13 of the Tribunals and Inquiries Act 1971 (subsection (1) of which provides that on a point of law an appeal shall lie to the High Court from a decision of any tribunal mentioned in that subsection or the tribunal may be required to state a case for the opinion of the High Court), insert the following new subsection after subsection (5)— *Further appeal on point of law.* *1971 c. 62.*

" (5A) Subsection (1) of this section shall apply to a decision of the Secretary of State on an appeal under section 41 of the Consumer Credit Act 1974 from a determination of the Director General of Fair Trading as it applies to a decision of any of the tribunals mentioned in that subsection, but with the substitution for the reference to a party to proceedings of a reference to any person who had a right to appeal to the Secretary of State (whether or not he has exercised that right) ; and accordingly references in subsections (1) and (3) of this section to a tribunal shall be construed, in relation to such an appeal, as references to the Secretary of State."

(2) In subsection (6)(*a*) of the said section 13 (application to Scotland), after the word " commissioners " there shall be inserted the words " or on an appeal under section 41 of the Consumer Credit Act 1974 by a company registered in Scotland or by any other person whose principal or prospective principal place of business in the United Kingdom is in Scotland ".

(3) In subsection (7) of the said section 13 (application to Northern Ireland) after " subsection (1) of this section " insert " and in relation to a decision of the Secretary of State on an appeal under section 41 of the Consumer Credit Act 1974 by a company registered in Northern Ireland or by any other person whose principal or prospective principal place of business in the United Kingdom is in Northern Ireland."

PART IV

SEEKING BUSINESS

Advertising

Advertise-
ments to
which
Part IV
applies.

43.—(1) This Part applies to any advertisement, published for the purposes of a business carried on by the advertiser, indicating that he is willing—

(*a*) to provide credit, or

(*b*) to enter into an agreement for the bailment or (in Scotland) the hiring of goods by him.

(2) An advertisement does not fall within subsection (1) if the advertiser does not carry on—

(*a*) a consumer credit business or consumer hire business, or

(*b*) a business in the course of which he provides credit to individuals secured on land, or

(*c*) a business which comprises or relates to unregulated agreements where—

(i) the proper law of the agreement is the law of a country outside the United Kingdom, and

(ii) if the proper law of the agreement were the law of a part of the United Kingdom it would be a regulated agreement.

(3) An advertisement does not fall within subsection (1)(*a*) if it indicates—

(*a*) that the credit must exceed £5,000, and that no security is required, or the security is to consist of property other than land, or

(*b*) that the credit is available only to a body corporate.

(4) An advertisement does not fall within subsection (1)(*b*) if it indicates that the advertiser is not willing to enter into a consumer hire agreement.

(5) The Secretary of State may by order provide that this Part shall not apply to other advertisements of a description specified in the order.

44.—(1) The Secretary of State shall make regulations as to the form and content of advertisements to which this Part applies, and the regulations shall contain such provisions as appear to him appropriate with a view to ensuring that, having Form and regard to its subject-matter and the amount of detail included in content of it, an advertisement conveys a fair and reasonably comprehensive advertise-indication of the nature of the credit or hire facilities offered ments. by the advertiser and of their true cost to persons using them.

(2) Regulations under subsection (1) may in particular—

(a) require specified information to be included in the prescribed manner in advertisements, and other speci-fied material to be excluded ;

(b) contain requirements to ensure that specified informa-tion is clearly brought to the attention of persons to whom advertisements are directed, and that one part of an advertisement is not given insufficient or exces-sive prominence compared with another.

45. If an advertisement to which this Part applies indicates Prohibition that the advertiser is willing to provide credit under a restricted- of advertise-use credit agreement relating to goods or services to be supplied ment where goods etc. by any person, but at the time when the advertisement is pub- not sold lished that person is not holding himself out as prepared to sell for cash.. the goods or provide the services (as the case may be) for cash, the advertiser commits an offence.

46.—(1) If an advertisement to which this Part applies conveys False or information which in a material respect is false or misleading misleading advertise-the advertiser commits an offence. ments.

(2) Information stating or implying an intention on the advertiser's part which he has not got is false.

47.—(1) Where an advertiser commits an offence against Advertising regulations made under section 44 or against section 45 or 46 infringements. or would be taken to commit such an offence but for the defence provided by section 168, a like offence is committed by—

(a) the publisher of the advertisement, and

(b) any person who, in the course of a business carried on by him, devised the advertisement, or a part of it rele-vant to the first-mentioned offence, and

(c) where the advertiser did not procure the publication of the advertisement, the person who did procure it.

(2) In proceedings for an offence under subsection (1)(a) it is a defence for the person charged to prove that—

(a) the advertisement was published in the course of a business carried on by him, and

B

PART IV
SEEKING
BUSINESS

(b) he received the advertisement in the course of that business, and did not know and had no reason to suspect that its publication would be an offence under this Part.

Canvassing etc.

Definition of canvassing off trade premises (regulated agreements).

48.—(1) An individual (the " canvasser ") canvasses a regulated agreement off trade premises if he solicits the entry (as debtor or hirer) of another individual (the " consumer ") into the agreement by making oral representations to the consumer, or any other individual, during a visit by the canvasser to any place (not excluded by subsection (2)) where the consumer, or that other individual, as the case may be, is, being a visit—

(a) carried out for the purpose of making such oral representations to individuals who are at that place, but

(b) not carried out in response to a request made on a previous occasion.

(2) A place is excluded from subsection (1) if it is a place where a business is carried on (whether on a permanent or temporary basis) by—

(a) the creditor or owner, or

(b) a supplier, or

(c) the canvasser, or the person whose employee or agent the canvasser is, or

(d) the consumer.

Prohibition of canvassing debtor-creditor agreements off trade premises.

49.—(1) It is an offence to canvass debtor-creditor agreements off trade premises.

(2) It is also an offence to solicit the entry of an individual (as debtor) into a debtor-creditor agreement during a visit carried out in response to a request made on a previous occasion, where—

(a) the request was not in writing signed by or on behalf of the person making it, and

(b) if no request for the visit had been made, the soliciting would have constituted the canvassing of a debtor-creditor agreement off trade premises.

(3) Subsections (1) and (2) do not apply to any soliciting for an agreement enabling the debtor to overdraw on a current account of any description kept with the creditor, where—

(a) the Director has determined that current accounts of that description kept with the creditor are excluded from subsections (1) and (2), and

(b) the debtor already keeps an account with the creditor (whether a current account or not).

(4) A determination under subsection (3)(a)—

(a) may be made subject to such conditions as the Director thinks fit, and

(b) shall be made only where the Director is of opinion that it is not against the interests of debtors.

(5) If soliciting is done in breach of a condition imposed under subsection (4)(a), the determination under subsection (3)(a) does not apply to it.

50.—(1) A person commits an offence who, with a view to financial gain, sends to a minor any document inviting him to—

(a) borrow money, or

(b) obtain goods on credit or hire, or

(c) obtain services on credit, or

(d) apply for information or advice on borrowing money or otherwise obtaining credit, or hiring goods.

(2) In proceedings under subsection (1) in respect of the sending of a document to a minor, it is a defence for the person charged to prove that he did not know, and had no reasonable cause to suspect, that he was a minor.

(3) Where a document is received by a minor at any school or other educational establishment for minors, a person sending it to him at that establishment knowing or suspecting it to be such an establishment shall be taken to have reasonable cause to suspect that he is a minor.

51.—(1) It is an offence to give a person a credit-token if he has not asked for it.

(2) To comply with subsection (1) a request must be contained in a document signed by the person making the request, unless the credit-token agreement is a small debtor-creditor-supplier agreement.

(3) Subsection (1) does not apply to the giving of a credit-token to a person—

(a) for use under a credit-token agreement already made, or

(b) in renewal or replacement of a credit-token previously accepted by him under a credit-token agreement which continues in force, whether or not varied.

Miscellaneous

52.—(1) Regulations may be made—

(*a*) as to the form and content of any document (a " quotation ") by which a person who carries on a consumer credit business or consumer hire business, or a business in the course of which he provides credit to individuals secured on land, gives prospective customers information about the terms on which he is prepared to do business ;

(*b*) requiring a person carrying on such a business to provide quotations to such persons and in such circumstances as are prescribed.

(2) Regulations under subsection (1)(*a*) may in particular contain provisions relating to quotations such as are set out in relation to advertisements in section 44.

53. Regulations may require a person who carries on a consumer credit business or consumer hire business, or a business in the course of which he provides credit to individuals secured on land, to display in the prescribed manner, at any premises where the business is carried on to which the public have access, prescribed information about the business.

54. Without prejudice to the generality of section 26, regulations under that section may include provisions further regulating the seeking of business by a licensee who carries on a consumer credit business or a consumer hire business.

PART V

ENTRY INTO CREDIT OR HIRE AGREEMENTS

Preliminary matters

55.—(1) Regulations may require specified information to be disclosed in the prescribed manner to the debtor or hirer before a regulated agreement is made.

(2) A regulated agreement is not properly executed unless regulations under subsection (1) were complied with before the making of the agreement.

56.—(1) In this Act " antecedent negotiations " means any negotiations with the debtor or hirer—

(*a*) conducted by the creditor or owner in relation to the making of any regulated agreement, or

(b) conducted by a credit-broker in relation to goods sold or proposed to be sold by the credit-broker to the creditor before forming the subject-matter of a debtor-creditor-supplier agreement within section 12(a), or

(c) conducted by the supplier in relation to a transaction financed or proposed to be financed by a debtor-creditor-supplier agreement within section 12(b) or (c),

and " negotiator " means the person by whom negotiations are so conducted with the debtor or hirer.

(2) Negotiations with the debtor in a case falling within subsection (1)(b) or (c) shall be deemed to be conducted by the negotiator in the capacity of agent of the creditor as well as in his actual capacity.

(3) An agreement is void if, and to the extent that, it purports in relation to an actual or prospective regulated agreement—

(a) to provide that a person acting as, or on behalf of, a negotiator is to be treated as the agent of the debtor or hirer, or

(b) to relieve a person from liability for acts or omissions of any person acting as, or on behalf of, a negotiator.

(4) For the purposes of this Act, antecedent negotiations shall be taken to begin when the negotiator and the debtor or hirer first enter into communication (including communication by advertisement), and to include any representations made by the negotiator to the debtor or hirer and any other dealings between them.

57.—(1) The withdrawal of a party from a prospective regulated agreement shall operate to apply this Part to the agreement, any linked transaction and any other thing done in anticipation of the making of the agreement as it would apply if the agreement were made and then cancelled under section 69.

(2) The giving to a party of a written or oral notice which, however expressed, indicates the intention of the other party to withdraw from a prospective regulated agreement operates as a withdrawal from it.

(3) Each of the following shall be deemed to be the agent of the creditor or owner for the purpose of receiving a notice under subsection (2)—

(a) a credit-broker or supplier who is the negotiator in antecedent negotiations, and

(b) any person who, in the course of a business carried on by him, acts on behalf of the debtor or hirer in any negotiations for the agreement.

(4) Where the agreement, if made, would not be a cancellable agreement, subsection (1) shall nevertheless apply as if the contrary were the case.

Opportunity
for withdrawal
from
prospective
land
mortgage.

58.—(1) Before sending to the debtor or hirer, for his signature, an unexecuted agreement in a case where the prospective regulated agreement is to be secured on land (the " mortgaged land "), the creditor or owner shall give the debtor or hirer a copy of the unexecuted agreement which contains a notice in the prescribed form indicating the right of the debtor or hirer to withdraw from the prospective agreement, and how and when the right is exercisable, together with a copy of any other document referred to in the unexecuted agreement.

(2) Subsection (1) does not apply to—

> (a) a restricted-use credit agreement to finance the purchase of the mortgaged land, or

> (b) an agreement for a bridging loan in connection with the purchase of the mortgaged land or other land.

Agreement
to enter future
agreement
void.

59.—(1) An agreement is void if, and to the extent that, it purports to bind a person to enter as debtor or hirer into a prospective regulated agreement.

(2) Regulations may exclude from the operation of subsection (1) agreements such as are described in the regulations.

Making the agreement

Form and
content of
agreements.

60.—(1) The Secretary of State shall make regulations as to the form and content of documents embodying regulated agreements, and the regulations shall contain such provisions as appear to him appropriate with a view to ensuring that the debtor or hirer is made aware of—

> (a) the rights and duties conferred or imposed on him by the agreement,

> (b) the amount and rate of the total charge for credit (in the case of a consumer credit agreement),

> (c) the protection and remedies available to him under this Act, and

> (d) any other matters which, in the opinion of the Secretary of State, it is desirable for him to know about in connection with the agreement.

(2) Regulations under subsection (1) may in particular—

> (a) require specified information to be included in the prescribed manner in documents, and other specified material to be excluded ;

(*b*) contain requirements to ensure that specified information is clearly brought to the attention of the debtor or hirer, and that one part of a document is not given insufficient or excessive prominence compared with another.

(3) If, on an application made to the Director by a person carrying on a consumer credit business or a consumer hire business, it appears to the Director impracticable for the applicant to comply with any requirement of regulations under subsection (1) in a particular case, he may, by notice to the applicant direct that the requirement be waived or varied in relation to such agreements, and subject to such conditions (if any), as he may specify, and this Act and the regulations shall have effect accordingly.

(4) The Director shall give a notice under subsection (3) only if he is satisfied that to do so would not prejudice the interests of debtors or hirers.

61.—(1) A regulated agreement is not properly executed unless— *Signing of agreement.*

(*a*) a document in the prescribed form itself containing all the prescribed terms and conforming to regulations under section 60(1) is signed in the prescribed manner both by the debtor or hirer and by or on behalf of the creditor or owner, and

(*b*) the document embodies all the terms of the agreement, other than implied terms, and

(*c*) the document is, when presented or sent to the debtor or hirer for signature, in such a state that all its terms are readily legible.

(2) In addition, where the agreement is one to which section 58(1) applies, it is not properly executed unless—

(*a*) the requirements of section 58(1) were complied with, and

(*b*) the unexecuted agreement was sent, for his signature, to the debtor or hirer by post not less than seven days after a copy of it was given to him under section 58(1), and

(*c*) during the consideration period, the creditor or owner refrained from approaching the debtor or hirer (whether in person, by telephone or letter, or in any other way) except in response to a specific request made by the debtor or hirer after the beginning of the consideration period, and (*d*) no notice of withdrawal by the debtor or hirer was received by the creditor or owner before the sending of the unexecuted agreement.

(3) In subsection (2)(*c*), " the consideration period " means the period beginning with the giving of the copy under section 58(1) and ending—

(*a*) at the expiry of seven days after the day on which the unexecuted agreement is sent, for his signature, to the debtor or hirer, or

(*b*) on its return by the debtor or hirer after signature by him,

whichever first occurs.

(4) Where the debtor or hirer is a partnership or an unincorporated body of persons, subsection (1)(*a*) shall apply with the substitution for " by the debtor or hirer " of " by or on behalf of the debtor or hirer ".

Duty to supply copy of unexecuted agreement.

62.—(1) If the unexecuted agreement is presented personally to the debtor or hirer for his signature, but on the occasion when he signs it the document does not become an executed agreement, a copy of it, and of any other document referred to in it, must be there and then delivered to him.

(2) If the unexecuted agreement is sent to the debtor or hirer for his signature, a copy of it, and of any other document referred to in it, must be sent to him at the same time.

(3) A regulated agreement is not properly executed if the requirements of this section are not observed.

Duty to supply copy of executed agreement.

63.—(1) If the unexecuted agreement is presented personally to the debtor or hirer for his signature, and on the occasion when he signs it the document becomes an executed agreement, a copy of the executed agreement, and of any other document referred to in it, must be there and then delivered to him.

(2) A copy of the executed agreement, and of any other document referred to in it, must be given to the debtor or hirer within the seven days following the making of the agreement unless—

(*a*) subsection (1) applies, or

(*b*) the unexecuted agreement was sent to the debtor or hirer for his signature and, on the occasion of his signing it, the document became an executed agreement.

(3) In the case of a cancellable agreement, a copy under subsection (2) must be sent by post.

(4) In the case of a credit-token agreement, a copy under subsection (2) need not be given within the seven days following the making of the agreement if it is given before or at the time when the credit-token is given to the debtor.

(5) A regulated agreement is not properly executed if the requirements of this section are not observed.

64.—(1) In the case of a cancellable agreement, a notice in the prescribed form indicating the right of the debtor or hirer to cancel the agreement, how and when that right is exercisable, and the name and address of a person to whom notice of cancellation may be given,—

Duty to give notice of cancellation rights.

    (*a*) must be included in every copy given to the debtor or hirer under section 62 or 63, and

    (*b*) except where section 63(2) applied, must also be sent by post to the debtor or hirer within the seven days following the making of the agreement.

(2) In the case of a credit-token agreement, a notice under subsection (1)(*b*) need not be sent by post within the seven days following the making of the agreement if either—

    (*a*) it is sent by post to the debtor or hirer before the credit-token is given to him, or

    (*b*) it is sent by post to him together with the credit-token.

(3) Regulations may provide that except where section 63(2) applied a notice sent under subsection (1)(*b*) shall be accompanied by a further copy of the executed agreement, and of any other document referred to in it.

(4) Regulations may provide that subsection (1)(*b*) is not to apply in the case of agreements such as are described in the regulations, being agreements made by a particular person, if—

    (*a*) on an application by that person to the Director, the Director has determined that, having regard to—

        (i) the manner in which antecedent negotiations for agreements with the applicant of that description are conducted, and

        (ii) the information provided to debtors or hirers before such agreements are made,

    the requirement imposed by subsection (1)(*b*) can be dispensed with without prejudicing the interests of debtors or hirers ; and

    (*b*) any conditions imposed by the Director in making the determination are complied with.

(5) A cancellable agreement is not properly executed if the requirements of this section are not observed.

65.—(1) An improperly-executed regulated agreement is enforceable against the debtor or hirer on an order of the court only.

Consequences
of improper
execution.

(2) A retaking of goods or land to which a regulated agreement relates is an enforcement of the agreement.

Acceptance
of credit-
tokens.

66.—(1) The debtor shall not be liable under a credit-token agreement for use made of the credit-token by any person unless the debtor had previously accepted the credit-token, or the use constituted an acceptance of it by him.

(2) The debtor accepts a credit-token when—

    (*a*) it is signed , or

    (*b*) a receipt for it is signed, or

    (*c*) it is first used,

either by the debtor himself or by a person who, pursuant to the agreement, is authorised by him to use it.

Cancellation of certain agreements within cooling-off period

Cancellable
agreements.

67. A regulated agreement may be cancelled by the debtor or hirer in accordance with this Part if the antecedent negotiations included oral representations made when in the presence of the debtor or hirer by an individual acting as, or on behalf of, the negotiator, unless—

    (*a*) the agreement is secured on land, or is a restricted-use credit agreement to finance the purchase of land or is an agreement for a bridging loan in connection with the purchase of land, or

    (*b*) the unexecuted agreement is signed by the debtor or hirer at premises at which any of the following is carrying on any business (whether on a permanent or temporary basis)—

        (i) the creditor or owner ;

        (ii) any party to a linked transaction (other than the debtor or hirer or a relative of his) ;

        (iii) the negotiator in any antecedent negotiations.

Cooling-off
period.

68. The debtor or hirer may serve notice of cancellation of a cancellable agreement between his signing of the unexecuted agreement and—

    (*a*) the end of the fifth day following the day on which he received a copy under section 63(2) or a notice under section 64(1)(*b*), or (*b*) if (by virtue of regulations made under section 64(4)) section 64(1)(*b*) does not apply, the end of the fourteenth day following the day on which he signed the un-executed agreement.

69.—(1) If within the period specified in section 68 the debtor or hirer under a cancellable agreement serves on—

(*a*) the creditor or owner, or

(*b*) the person specified in the notice under section 64(1), or

(*c*) a person who (whether by virtue of subsection (6) or otherwise) is the agent of the creditor or owner,

a notice (a " notice of cancellation ") which, however expressed and whether or not conforming to the notice given under section 64(1), indicates the intention of the debtor or hirer to withdraw from the agreement, the notice shall operate—

(i) to cancel the agreement, and any linked transaction, and

(ii) to withdraw any offer by the debtor or hirer, or his relative, to enter into a linked transaction.

(2) In the case of a debtor-creditor-supplier agreement for restricted-use credit financing—

(*a*) the doing of work or supply of goods to meet an emergency, or

(*b*) the supply of goods which, before service of the notice of cancellation, had by the act of the debtor or his relative become incorporated in any land or thing not comprised in the agreement or any linked transaction,

subsection (1) shall apply with the substitution of the following for paragraph (i)—

" (i) to cancel only such provisions of the agreement and any linked transaction as—

(*aa*) relate to the provision of credit, or

(*bb*) require the debtor to pay an item in the total charge for credit, or

(*cc*) subject the debtor to any obligation other than to pay for the doing of the said work, or the supply of the said goods ".

(3) Except so far as is otherwise provided, references in this Act to the cancellation of an agreement or transaction do not include a case within subsection (2).

(4) Except as otherwise provided by or under this Act, an agreement or transaction cancelled under subsection (1) shall be treated as if it had never been entered into.

(5) Regulations may exclude linked transactions of the prescribed description from subsection (1)(i) or (ii).

(6) Each of the following shall be deemed to be the agent of the creditor or owner for the purpose of receiving a notice of cancellation—

(*a*) a credit-broker or supplier who is the negotiator in antecedent negotiations, and

(*b*) any person who, in the course of a business carried on by him, acts on behalf of the debtor or hirer in any negotiations for the agreement.

(7) Whether or not it is actually received by him, a notice of cancellation sent by post to a person shall be deemed to be served on him at the time of posting.

Cancellation:
recovery of
money paid
by debtor
or hirer.
70.—(1) On the cancellation of a regulated agreement, and of any linked transaction,—

(*a*) any sum paid by the debtor or hirer, or his relative, under or in contemplation of the agreement or trans-action, including any item in the total charge for credit, shall become repayable, and

(*b*) any sum, including any item in the total charge for credit, which but for the cancellation is, or would or might become, payable by the debtor or hirer, or his relative, under the agreement or transaction shall cease to be, or shall not become, so payable, and

(*c*) in the case of a debtor-creditor-supplier agreement fall-ing within section 12(*b*), any sum paid on the debtor's behalf by the creditor to the supplier shall become repayable to the creditor.

(2) If, under the terms of a cancelled agreement or trans-action, the debtor or hirer, or his relative, is in possession of any goods, he shall have a lien on them for any sum repayable to him under subsection (1) in respect of that agreement or transaction, or any other linked transaction.

(3) A sum repayable under subsection (1) is repayable by the person to whom it was originally paid, but in the case of a debtor-creditor-supplier agreement falling within section 12(*b*) the creditor and the supplier shall be under a joint and several liability to repay sums paid by the debtor, or his relative, under the agreement or under a linked transaction falling within section 19(1)(*b*) and accordingly, in such a case, the creditor shall be entitled, in accordance with rules of court, to have the supplier made a party to any proceedings brought against the creditor to recover any such sums.

(4) Subject to any agreement between them, the creditor shall be entitled to be indemnified by the supplier for loss suffered by the creditor in satisfying his liability under sub- section (3), including costs reasonably incurred by him in defending proceedings instituted by the debtor.

(5) Subsection (1) does not apply to any sum which, if not paid by a debtor, would be payable by virtue of section 71, and applies to a sum paid or payable by a debtor for the issue of a credit-token only where the credit-token has been returned to the creditor or surrendered to a supplier.

(6) If the total charge for credit includes an item in respect of a fee or commission charged by a credit-broker, the amount repayable under subsection (1) in respect of that item shall be the excess over £1 of the fee or commission.

(7) If the total charge for credit includes any sum payable or paid by the debtor to a credit-broker otherwise than in respect of a fee or commission charged by him, that sum shall for the purposes of subsection (6) be treated as if it were such a fee or commission.

(8) So far only as is necessary to give effect to section 69(2), this section applies to an agreement or transaction within that subsection as it applies to a cancelled agreement or transaction.

71.—(1) Notwithstanding the cancellation of a regulated con- Cancellation: sumer credit agreement, other than a debtor-creditor-supplier repayment agreement for restricted-use credit, the agreement shall continue of credit. in force so far as it relates to repayment of credit and payment of interest.

(2) If, following the cancellation of a regulated consumer credit agreement, the debtor repays the whole or a portion of the credit—

(a) before the expiry of one month following service of the notice of cancellation, or

(b) in the case of a credit repayable by instalments, before the date on which the first instalment is due,

no interest shall be payable on the amount repaid.

(3) If the whole of a credit repayable by instalments is not repaid on or before the date specified in subsection (2)(b), the debtor shall not be liable to repay any of the credit except on receipt of a request in writing in the prescribed form, signed by or on behalf of the creditor, stating the amounts of the remaining instalments (recalculated by the creditor as nearly as may be in accordance with the agreement and without extending the repayment period), but excluding any sum other than principal and interest.

(4) Repayment of a credit, or payment of interest, under a cancelled agreement shall be treated as duly made if it is made to any person on whom, under section 69, a notice of cancellation could have been served, other than a person referred to in section 69(6)(*b*).

Cancellation:
return of
goods.

72.—(1) This section applies where any agreement or transaction relating to goods, being—

> (*a*) a restricted-use debtor-creditor-supplier agreement, a consumer hire agreement, or a linked transaction to which the debtor or hirer under any regulated agreement is a party, or
>
> (*b*) a linked transaction to which a relative of the debtor or hirer under any regulated agreement is a party,

is cancelled after the debtor or hirer (in a case within paragraph (*a*)) or the relative (in a case within paragraph (*b*)) has acquired possession of the goods by virtue of the agreement or transaction.

(2) In this section—

> (*a*) " the possessor " means the person who has acquired possession of the goods as mentioned in subsection (1),
>
> (*b*) " the other party " means the person from whom the possessor acquired possession, and
>
> (*c*) " the pre-cancellation period " means the period beginning when the possessor acquired possession and ending with the cancellation.

(3) The possessor shall be treated as having been under a duty throughout the pre-cancellation period—

> (*a*) to retain possession of the goods, and
>
> (*b*) to take reasonable care of them.

(4) On the cancellation, the possessor shall be under a duty, subject to any lien, to restore the goods to the other party in accordance with this section, and meanwhile to retain possession of the goods and take reasonable care of them.

(5) The possessor shall not be under any duty to deliver the goods except at his own premises and in pursuance of a request in writing signed by or on behalf of the other party and served on the possessor either before, or at the time when, the goods are collected from those premises.

(6) If the possessor—

> (*a*) delivers the goods (whether at his own premises or elsewhere) to any person on whom, under section 69, a notice of cancellation could have been served (other than a person referred to in section 69(6)(*b*)), or

(*b*) sends the goods at his own expense to such a person,
he shall be discharged from any duty to retain the goods or
deliver them to any person.

(7) Where the possessor delivers the goods as mentioned
in subsection (6)(*a*), his obligation to take care of the goods
shall cease ; and if he sends the goods as mentioned in subsection (6)(*b*), he shall be under a duty to take reasonable care to
see that they are received by the other party and not damaged
in transit, but in other respects his duty to take care of the
goods shall cease.

(8) Where, at any time during the period of 21 days following
the cancellation, the possessor receives such a request as is
mentioned in subsection (5), and unreasonably refuses or
unreasonably fails to comply with it, his duty to take reasonable care of the goods shall continue until he delivers or sends
the goods as mentioned in subsection (6), but if within that
period he does not receive such a request his duty to take
reasonable care of the goods shall cease at the end of that period.

(9) The preceding provisions of this section do not apply to—
   (*a*) perishable goods, or
   (*b*) goods which by their nature are consumed by use and
        which, before the cancellation, were so consumed, or
   (*c*) goods supplied to meet an emergency, or
   (*d*) goods which, before the cancellation, had become
        incorporated in any land or thing not comprised in
        the cancelled agreement or a linked transaction.

(10) Where the address of the possessor is specified in the
executed agreement, references in this section to his own
premises are to that address and no other.

(11) Breach of a duty imposed by this section is actionable
as a breach of statutory duty.

73.—(1) This section applies on the cancellation of a regu- Cancellation:
lated agreement where, in antecedent negotiations, the negotiator goods given in
agreed to take goods in part-exchange (the " part-exchange part-exchange.
goods ") and those goods have been delivered to him.

(2) Unless, before the end of the period of ten days beginning
with the date of cancellation, the part-exchange goods are
returned to the debtor or hirer in a condition substantially as
good as when they were delivered to the negotiator, the debtor
or hirer shall be entitled to recover from the negotiator a sum
equal to the part-exchange allowance (as defined in subsection
(7)(*b*)).

(3) In the case of a debtor-creditor-supplier agreement within section 12(*b*), the negotiator and the creditor shall be under a joint and several liability to pay to the debtor a sum recoverable under subsection (2).

(4) Subject to any agreement between them, the creditor shall be entitled to be indemnified by the negotiator for loss suffered by the creditor in satisfying his liability under subsection (3), including costs reasonably incurred by him in defending proceedings instituted by the debtor.

(5) During the period of ten days beginning with the date of cancellation, the debtor or hirer, if he is in possession of goods to which the cancelled agreement relates, shall have a lien on them for—

(*a*) delivery of the part-exchange goods, in a condition substantially as good as when they were delivered to the negotiator, or

(*b*) a sum equal to the part-exchange allowance ;

and if the lien continues to the end of that period it shall thereafter subsist only as a lien for a sum equal to the part-exchange allowance.

(6) Where the debtor or hirer recovers from the negotiator or creditor, or both of them jointly, a sum equal to the part-exchange allowance, then, if the title of the debtor or hirer to the part-exchange goods has not vested in the negotiator, it shall so vest on the recovery of that sum.

(7) For the purposes of this section—

(*a*) the negotiator shall be treated as having agreed to take goods in part-exchange if, in pursuance of the antecedent negotiations, he either purchased or agreed to purchase those goods or accepted or agreed to accept them as part of the consideration for the cancelled agreement, and

(*b*) the part-exchange allowance shall be the sum agreed as such in the antecedent negotiations or, if no such agreement was arrived at, such sum as it would have been reasonable to allow in respect of the part-exchange goods if no notice of cancellation had been served.

(8) In an action brought against the creditor for a sum recoverable under subsection (2), he shall be entitled, in accordance with rules of court, to have the negotiator made a party to the proceedings.

Exclusion of certain agreements from Part V

74.—(1) This Part (except section 56) does not apply to—

(*a*) a non-commercial agreement, or

(*b*) a debtor-creditor agreement enabling the debtor to overdraw on a current account, or

(c) a debtor-creditor agreement to finance the making of
such payments arising on, or connected with, the death
of a person as may be prescribed.

PART V
ENTRY INTO
AGREE-
MENTS

(2) This Part (except sections 55 and 56) does not apply to
a small debtor-creditor-supplier agreement for restricted-use
credit.

(3) Subsection (1)(b) or (c) applies only where the Director so
determines, and such a determination—

(a) may be made subject to such conditions as the Director
thinks fit, and

(b) shall be made only if the Director is of opinion that
it is not against the interests of debtors.

(4) If any term of an agreement falling within subsection
(1)(b) or (c) or (2) is expressed in writing, regulations under
section 60(1) shall apply to that term (subject to section 60(3))
as if the agreement were a regulated agreement not falling
within subsection (1)(b) or (c) or (2).

PART VI

MATTERS ARISING DURING CURRENCY OF CREDIT OR HIRE AGREEMENTS

75.—(1) If the debtor under a debtor-creditor-supplier agreement falling within section 12(b) or (c) has, in relation to a transaction financed by the agreement, any claim against the supplier
in respect of a misrepresentation or breach of contract, he shall
have a like claim against the creditor, who, with the supplier,
shall accordingly be jointly and severally liable to the debtor.

Liability
of creditor
for breaches
by supplier.

(2) Subject to any agreement between them, the creditor shall
be entitled to be indemnified by the supplier for loss suffered by
the creditor in satisfying his liability under subsection (1),
including costs reasonably incurred by him in defending
proceedings instituted by the debtor.

(3) Subsection (1) does not apply to a claim—
(a) under a non-commercial agreement, or
(b) so far as the claim relates to any single item to which
the supplier has attached a cash price not exceeding
£30 or more than £10,000.

(4) This section applies notwithstanding that the debtor, in
entering into the transaction, exceeded the credit limit or otherwise contravened any term of the agreement.

(5) In an action brought against the creditor under subsection
(1) he shall be entitled, in accordance with rules of court, to
have the supplier made a party to the proceedings.

Duty to give
notice before
taking certain
action.

76.—(1) The creditor or owner is not entitled to enforce a term of a regulated agreement by—

(a) demanding earlier payment of any sum, or

(b) recovering possession of any goods or land, or

(c) treating any right conferred on the debtor or hirer by the agreement as terminated, restricted or deferred,

except by or after giving the debtor or hirer not less than seven days' notice of his intention to do so.

(2) Subsection (1) applies only where—

(a) a period for the duration of the agreement is specified in the agreement, and

(b) that period has not ended when the creditor or owner does an act mentioned in subsection (1),

but so applies notwithstanding that, under the agreement, any party is entitled to terminate it before the end of the period so specified.

(3) A notice under subsection (1) is ineffective if not in the prescribed form.

(4) Subsection (1) does not prevent a creditor from treating the right to draw on any credit as restricted or deferred and taking such steps as may be necessary to make the restriction or deferment effective.

(5) Regulations may provide that subsection (1) is not to apply to agreements described by the regulations.

(6) Subsection (1) does not apply to a right of enforcement arising by reason of any breach by the debtor or hirer of the regulated agreement.

Duty to give
information to
debtor under
fixed-sum
credit
agreement.

77.—(1) The creditor under a regulated agreement for fixed-sum credit, within the prescribed period after receiving a request in writing to that effect from the debtor and payment of a fee of 15 new pence, shall give the debtor a copy of the executed agreement (if any) and of any other document referred to in it, together with a statement signed by or on behalf of the creditor showing, according to the information to which it is practicable for him to refer,—

(a) the total sum paid under the agreement by the debtor ;

(b) the total sum which has become payable under the agreement by the debtor but remains unpaid, and the various amounts comprised in that total sum, with the date when each became due ; and

(c) the total sum which is to become payable under the agreement by the debtor, and the various amounts comprised in that total sum, with the date, or mode of determining the date, when each becomes due.

(2) If the creditor possesses insufficient information to enable him to ascertain the amounts and dates mentioned in subsection (1)(c), he shall be taken to comply with that paragraph if his statement under subsection (1) gives the basis on which, under the regulated agreement, they would fall to be ascertained.

(3) Subsection (1) does not apply to—

(a) an agreement under which no sum is, or will or may become, payable by the debtor, or

(b) a request made less than one month after a previous request under that subsection relating to the same agreement was complied with.

(4) If the creditor under an agreement fails to comply with subsection (1)—

(a) he is not entitled, while the default continues, to enforce the agreement ; and

(b) if the default continues for one month he commits an offence.

(5) This section does not apply to a non-commercial agreement.

78.—(1) The creditor under a regulated agreement for running-account credit, within the prescribed period after receiving a request in writing to that effect from the debtor and payment of a fee of 15 new pence, shall give the debtor a copy of the executed agreement (if any) and of any other document referred to in it, together with a statement signed by or on behalf of the creditor showing, according to the information to which it is practicable for him to refer,—

(a) the state of the account, and

(b) the amount, if any, currently payable under the agreement by the debtor to the creditor, and

(c) the amounts and due dates of any payments which, if the debtor does not draw further on the account, will later become payable under the agreement by the debtor to the creditor.

(2) If the creditor possesses insufficient information to enable him to ascertain the amounts and dates mentioned in subsection (1)(c), he shall be taken to comply with that paragraph if his statement under subsection (1) gives the basis on which, under the regulated agreement, they would fall to be ascertained.

(3) Subsection (1) does not apply to—

    (a) an agreement under which no sum is, or will or may become, payable by the debtor, or

    (b) a request made less than one month after a previous request under that subsection relating to the same agreement was complied with.

(4) Where running-account credit is provided under a regulated agreement, the creditor shall give the debtor statements in the prescribed form, and with the prescribed contents—

    (a) showing according to the information to which it is practicable for him to refer, the state of the account at regular intervals of not more than twelve months, and

    (b) where the agreement provides, in relation to specified periods, for the making of payments by the debtor, or the charging against him of interest or any other sum, showing according to the information to which it is practicable for him to refer the state of the account at the end of each of those periods during which there is any movement in the account.

(5) A statement under subsection (4) shall be given within the prescribed period after the end of the period to which the statement relates.

(6) If the creditor under an agreement fails to comply with subsection (1)—

    (a) he is not entitled, while the default continues, to enforce the agreement ; and

    (b) if the default continues for one month he commits an offence.

(7) This section does not apply to a non-commercial agreement, and subsections (4) and (5) do not apply to a small agreement.

Duty to
give hirer
information.

79.—(1) The owner under a regulated consumer hire agreement, within the prescribed period after receiving a request in writing to that effect from the hirer and payment of a fee of 15 new pence, shall give to the hirer a copy of the executed agreement and of any other document referred to in it, together with a statement signed by or on behalf of the owner showing, according to the information to which it is practicable for him to refer, the total sum which has become payable under the agreement by the hirer but remains unpaid and the various amounts comprised in that total sum, with the date when each became due.

(2) Subsection (1) does not apply to—

    (*a*) an agreement under which no sum is, or will or may become, payable by the hirer, or

    (*b*) a request made less than one month after a previous request under that subsection relating to the same agreement was complied with.

(3) If the owner under an agreement fails to comply with subsection (1)—

    (*a*) he is not entitled, while the default continues, to enforce the agreement ; and

    (*b*) if the default continues for one month he commits an offence.

(4) This section does not apply to a non-commercial agreement.

80.—(1) Where a regulated agreement, other than a non-commercial agreement, requires the debtor or hirer to keep goods to which the agreement relates in his possession or control, he shall, within seven working days after he has received a request in writing to that effect from the creditor or owner, tell the creditor or owner where the goods are.

(2) If the debtor or hirer fails to comply with subsection (1), and the default continues for 14 days, he commits an offence.

81.—(1) Where a debtor or hirer is liable to make to the same person payments in respect of two or more regulated agreements, he shall be entitled, on making any payment in respect of the agreements which is not sufficient to discharge the total amount then due under all the agreements, to appropriate the sum so paid by him—

    (*a*) in or towards the satisfaction of the sum due under any one of the agreements, or

    (*b*) in or towards the satisfaction of the sums due under any two or more of the agreements in such proportions as he thinks fit.

(2) If the debtor or hirer fails to make any such appropriation where one or more of the agreements is—

    (*a*) a hire-purchase agreement or conditional sale agreement, or

    (*b*) a consumer hire agreement, or

    (*c*) an agreement in relation to which any security is provided,

the payment shall be appropriated towards the satisfaction of the sums due under the several agreements respectively in the proportions which those sums bear to one another.

PART VI
CURRENCY
OF AGREE-
MENTS
Variation of
agreements.

82.—(1) Where, under a power contained in a regulated agreement, the creditor or owner varies the agreement, the variation shall not take effect before notice of it is given to the debtor or hirer in the prescribed manner.

(2) Where an agreement (a " modifying agreement ") varies or supplements an earlier agreement, the modifying agreement shall for the purposes of this Act be treated as—

(*a*) revoking the earlier agreement, and

(*b*) containing provisions reproducing the combined effect of the two agreements,

and obligations outstanding in relation to the earlier agreement shall accordingly be treated as outstanding instead in relation to the modifying agreement.

(3) If the earlier agreement is a regulated agreement but (apart from this subsection) the modifying agreement is not then, unless the modifying agreement is for running-account credit, it shall be treated as a regulated agreement.

(4) If the earlier agreement is a regulated agreement for running-account credit, and by the modifying agreement the creditor allows the credit limit to be exceeded but intends the excess to be merely temporary, Part V (except section 56) shall not apply to the modifying agreement.

(5) If—

(*a*) the earlier agreement is a cancellable agreement, and

(*b*) the modifying agreement is made within the period applicable under section 68 to the earlier agreement,

then, whether or not the modifying agreement would, apart from this subsection, be a cancellable agreement, it shall be treated as a cancellable agreement in respect of which a notice may be served under section 68 not later than the end of the period applicable under that section to the earlier agreement.

(6) Except under subsection (5), a modifying agreement shall not be treated as a cancellable agreement.

(7) This section does not apply to a non-commercial agreement.

83.—(1) The debtor under a regulated consumer credit agreement shall not be liable to the creditor for any loss arising from use of the credit facility by another person not acting, or to be treated as acting, as the debtor's agent.

(2) This section does not apply to a non-commercial agreement, or to any loss in so far as it arises from misuse of an instrument to which section 4 of the Cheques Act 1957 applies.

84.—(1) Section 83 does not prevent the debtor under a credit-token agreement from being made liable to the extent of £30 (or the credit limit if lower) for loss to the creditor arising from use of the credit-token by other persons during a period beginning when the credit-token ceases to be in the possession of any authorised person and ending when the credit-token is once more in the possession of an authorised person.

(2) Section 83 does not prevent the debtor under a credit-token agreement from being made liable to any extent for loss to the creditor from use of the credit-token by a person who acquired possession of it with the debtor's consent.

(3) Subsections (1) and (2) shall not apply to any use of the credit-token after the creditor has been given oral or written notice that it is lost or stolen, or is for any other reason liable to misuse.

(4) Subsections (1) and (2) shall not apply unless there are contained in the credit-token agreement in the prescribed manner particulars of the name, address and telephone number of a person stated to be the person to whom notice is to be given under subsection (3).

(5) Notice under subsection (3) takes effect when received, but where it is given orally, and the agreement so requires, it shall be treated as not taking effect if not confirmed in writing within seven days.

(6) Any sum paid by the debtor for the issue of the credit-token, to the extent (if any) that it has not been previously offset by use made of the credit-token, shall be treated as paid towards satisfaction of any liability under subsection (1) or (2).

(7) The debtor, the creditor, and any person authorised by the debtor to use the credit-token, shall be authorised persons for the purposes of subsection (1).

(8) Where two or more credit-tokens are given under one credit-token agreement, the preceding provisions of this section apply to each credit-token separately.

85.—(1) Whenever, in connection with a credit-token agreement, a credit-token (other than the first) is given by the creditor to the debtor, the creditor shall give the debtor a copy of the executed agreement (if any) and of any other document referred to in it.

(2) If the creditor fails to comply with this section—

    (a) he is not entitled, while the default continues, to enforce the agreement ; and (*b*) if the default continues for one month he commits an offence.

(3) This section does not apply to a small agreement.

Death of
debtor or
hirer.

86.—(1) The creditor or owner under a regulated agreement is not entitled, by reason of the death of the debtor or hirer, to do an act specified in paragraphs (*a*) to (*e*) of section 87(1) if at the death the agreement is fully secured.

(2) If at the death of the debtor or hirer a regulated agreement is only partly secured or is unsecured, the creditor or owner is entitled, by reason of the death of the debtor or hirer, to do an act specified in paragraphs (*a*) to (*e*) of section 87(1) on an order of the court only.

(3) This section applies in relation to the termination of an agreement only where—

(*a*) a period for its duration is specified in the agreement, and

(*b*) that period has not ended when the creditor or owner purports to terminate the agreement,

but so applies notwithstanding that, under the agreement, any party is entitled to terminate it before the end of the period so specified.

(4) This section does not prevent the creditor from treating the right to draw on any credit as restricted or deferred, and taking such steps as may be necessary to make the restriction or deferment effective.

(5) This section does not affect the operation of any agreement providing for payment of sums—

(*a*) due under the regulated agreement, or

(*b*) becoming due under it on the death of the debtor or hirer,

out of the proceeds of a policy of assurance on his life.

(6) For the purposes of this section an act is done by reason of the death of the debtor or hirer if it is done under a power conferred by the agreement which is—

(*a*) exercisable on his death, or

(*b*) exercisable at will and exercised at any time after his death.

PART VII

DEFAULT AND TERMINATION

Default notices

87.—(1) Service of a notice on the debtor or hirer in accord- Need for
ance with section 88 (a " default notice ") is necessary before the default
creditor or owner can become entitled, by reason of any breach notice.
by the debtor or hirer of a regulated agreement,—

   (*a*) to terminate the agreement, or

   (*b*) to demand earlier payment of any sum, or

   (*c*) to recover possession of any goods or land, or

   (*d*) to treat any right conferred on the debtor or hirer by
        the agreement as terminated, restricted or deferred, or

   (*e*) to enforce any security.

(2) Subsection (1) does not prevent the creditor from treating
the right to draw upon any credit as restricted or deferred, and
taking such steps as may be necessary to make the restriction
or deferment effective.

(3) The doing of an act by which a floating charge becomes
fixed is not enforcement of a security.

(4) Regulations may provide that subsection (1) is not to
apply to agreements described by the regulations.

88.—(1) The default notice must be in the prescribed form Contents
and specify—   and effect
                                                               of default
   (*a*) the nature of the alleged breach ;   notice.

   (*b*) if the breach is capable of remedy, what action is
        required to remedy it and the date before which that
        action is to be taken ;

   (*c*) if the breach is not capable of remedy, the sum (if
        any) required to be paid as compensation for the
        breach, and the date before which it is to be paid.

(2) A date specified under subsection (1) must not be less
than seven days after the date of service of the default notice,
and the creditor or owner shall not take action such as is
mentioned in section 87(1) before the date so specified or (if
no requirement is made under subsection (1)) before those
seven days have elapsed.

(3) The default notice must not treat as a breach failure to
comply with a provision of the agreement which becomes
operative only on breach of some other provision, but if the
breach of that other provision is not duly remedied or compensation demanded under subsection (1) is not duly paid, or

PART VII
DEFAULT
AND TERMI-
NATION

(where no requirement is made under subsection (1)) if the seven days mentioned in subsection (2) have elapsed, the creditor or owner may treat the failure as a breach and section 87(1) shall not apply to it.

(4) The default notice must contain information in the prescribed terms about the consequences of failure to comply with it.

(5) A default notice making a requirement under subsection (1) may include a provision for the taking of action such as is mentioned in section 87(1) at any time after the restriction imposed by subsection (2) will cease, together with a statement that the provision will be ineffective if the breach is duly remedied or the compensation duly paid.

Compliance
with default
notice.

89. If before the date specified for that purpose in the default notice the debtor or hirer takes the action specified under section 88(1)(*b*) or (*c*) the breach shall be treated as not having occurred.

Further restriction of remedies for default

Retaking
of protected
hire-purchase
etc. goods.

90.—(1) At any time when—

(*a*) the debtor is in breach of a regulated hire-purchase or a regulated conditional sale agreement relating to goods, and

(*b*) the debtor has paid to the creditor one-third or more of the total price of the goods, and

(*c*) the property in the goods remains in the creditor,

the creditor is not entitled to recover possession of the goods from the debtor except on an order of the court.

(2) Where under a hire-purchase or conditional sale agreement the creditor is required to carry out any installation and the agreement specifies, as part of the total price, the amount to be paid in respect of the installation (the " installation charge ") the reference in subsection (1)(*b*) to one-third of the total price shall be construed as a reference to the aggregate of the installation charge and one-third of the remainder of the total price.

(3) In a case where—

(*a*) subsection (1)(*a*) is satisfied, but not subsection (1)(*b*), and

(*b*) subsection (1)(*b*) was satisfied on a previous occasion in relation to an earlier agreement, being a regulated hire-purchase or regulated conditional sale agreement, between the same parties, and relating to any of the goods comprised in the later agreement (whether or not other goods were also included),

subsection (1) shall apply to the later agreement with the omission of paragraph (*b*).

(4) If the later agreement is a modifying agreement, subsection (3) shall apply with the substitution, for the second reference to the later agreement, of a reference to the modifying agreement.

(5) Subsection (1) shall not apply, or shall cease to apply, to an agreement if the debtor has terminated, or terminates, the agreement.

(6) Where subsection (1) applies to an agreement at the death of the debtor, it shall continue to apply (in relation to the possessor of the goods) until the grant of probate or administration, or (in Scotland) confirmation (on which the personal representative would fall to be treated as the debtor).

(7) Goods falling within this section are in this Act referred to as " protected goods ".

91. If goods are recovered by the creditor in contravention of section 90—

> (*a*) the regulated agreement, if not previous terminated, shall terminate, and
>
> (*b*) the debtor shall be released from all liability under the agreement, and shall be entitled to recover from the creditor all sums paid by the debtor under the agreement.

Consequences of breach of s. 90.

92.—(1) Except under an order of the court, the creditor or owner shall not be entitled to enter any premises to take possession of goods subject to a regulated hire-purchase agreement, regulated conditional sale agreement or regulated consumer hire agreement.

Recovery of possession of goods or land.

(2) At any time when the debtor is in breach of a regulated conditional sale agreement relating to land, the creditor is entitled to recover possession of the land from the debtor, or any person claiming under him, on an order of the court only.

(3) An entry in contravention of subsection (1) or (2) is actionable as a breach of statutory duty.

93. The debtor under a regulated consumer credit agreement shall not be obliged to pay interest on sums which, in breach of the agreement, are unpaid by him at a rate—

> (*a*) where the total charge for credit includes an item in respect of interest, exceeding the rate of that interest, or

Interest not to be increased on default.

(b) in any other case, exceeding what would be the rate of the total charge for credit if any items included in the total charge for credit by virtue of section 20(2) were disregarded.

Early payment by debtor

Right to
complete
payments
ahead of time.

94.—(1) The debtor under a regulated consumer credit agreement is entitled at any time, by notice to the creditor and the payment to the creditor of all amounts payable by the debtor to him under the agreement (less any rebate allowable under section 95), to discharge the debtor's indebtedness under the agreement.

(2) A notice under subsection (1) may embody the exercise by the debtor of any option to purchase goods conferred on him by the agreement, and deal with any other matter arising on, or in relation to, the termination of the agreement.

Rebate
on early
settlement.

95.—(1) Regulations may provide for the allowance of a rebate of charges for credit to the debtor under a regulated consumer credit agreement where, under section 94, on refinancing, on breach of the agreement, or for any other reason, his indebtedness is discharged or becomes payable before the time fixed by the agreement, or any sum becomes payable by him before the time so fixed.

(2) Regulations under subsection (1) may provide for calculation of the rebate by reference to any sums paid or payable by the debtor or his relative under or in connection with the agreement (whether to the creditor or some other person), including sums under linked transactions and other items in the total charge for credit.

Effect on
linked
transactions.

96.—(1) Where for any reason the indebtedness of the debtor under a regulated consumer credit agreement is discharged before the time fixed by the agreement, he, and any relative of his, shall at the same time be discharged from any liability under a linked transaction, other than a debt which has already become payable.

(2) Subsection (1) does not apply to a linked transaction which is itself an agreement providing the debtor or his relative with credit.

(3) Regulations may exclude linked transactions of the prescribed description from the operation of subsection (1).

Duty to give
information.

97.—(1) The creditor under a regulated consumer credit agreement, within the prescribed period after he has received a request in writing to that effect from the debtor, shall give

the debtor a statement in the prescribed form indicating, according to the information to which it is practicable for him to
refer, the amount of the payment required to discharge the
debtor's indebtedness under the agreement, together with the
prescribed particulars showing how the amount is arrived at.

(2) Subsection (1) does not apply to a request made less than
one month after a previous request under that subsection relating
to the same agreement was complied with.

(3) If the creditor fails to comply with subsection (1)—

(*a*) he is not entitled, while the default continues, to enforce
the agreement ; and

(*b*) if the default continues for one month he commits an
offence.

Termination of agreements

98.—(1) The creditor or owner is not entitled to terminate Duty to give
a regulated agreement except by or after giving the debtor or notice of
hirer not less than seven days' notice of the termination. termination
(non-default
(2) Subsection (1) applies only where— cases).

(*a*) a period for the duration of the agreement is specified
in the agreement, and

(*b*) that period has not ended when the creditor or owner
does an act mentioned in subsection (1),

but so applies notwithstanding that, under the agreement, any
party is entitled to terminate it before the end of the period so
specified.

(3) A notice under subsection (1) is ineffective if not in the
prescribed form.

(4) Subsection (1) does not prevent a creditor from treating
the right to draw on any credit as restricted or deferred and
taking such steps as may be necessary to make the restriction
or deferment effective.

(5) Regulations may provide that subsection (1) is not to apply
to agreements described by the regulations.

(6) Subsection (1) does not apply to the termination of a
regulated agreement by reason of any breach by the debtor or
hirer of the agreement.

99.—(1) At any time before the final payment by the debtor Right to
under a regulated hire-purchase or regulated conditional sale terminate
agreement falls due, the debtor shall be entitled to terminate hire-purchase
the agreement by giving notice to any person entitled or etc. agreements.
authorised to receive the sums payable under the agreement.

(2) Termination of an agreement under subsection (1) does not affect any liability under the agreement which has accrued before the termination.

(3) Subsection (1) does not apply to a conditional sale agreement relating to land after the title to the land has passed to the debtor.

(4) In the case of a conditional sale agreement relating to goods, where the property in the goods, having become vested in the debtor, is transferred to a person who does not become the debtor under the agreement, the debtor shall not thereafter be entitled to terminate the agreement under subsection (1).

(5) Subject to subsection (4), where a debtor under a conditional sale agreement relating to goods terminates the agreement under this section after the property in the goods has become vested in him, the property in the goods shall thereupon vest in the person (the " previous owner ") in whom it was vested immediately before it became vested in the debtor:

Provided that if the previous owner has died, or any other event has occurred whereby that property, if vested in him immediately before that event, would thereupon have vested in some other person, the property shall be treated as having devolved as if it had been vested in the previous owner immediately before his death or immediately before that event, as the case may be.

Liability of
debtor on
termination of
hire-purchase
etc. agreement.

100.—(1) Where a regulated hire-purchase or regulated conditional sale agreement is terminated under section 99 the debtor shall be liable, unless the agreement provides for a smaller payment, or does not provide for any payment, to pay to the creditor the amount (if any) by which one-half of the total price exceeds the aggregate of the sums paid and the sums due in respect of the total price immediately before the termination.

(2) Where under a hire-purchase or conditional sale agreement the creditor is required to carry out any installation and the agreement specifies, as part of the total price, the amount to be paid in respect of the installation(the " installation charge ") the reference in subsection (1) to one-half of the total price shall be construed as a reference to the aggregate of the installation charge and one-half of the remainder of the total price.

(3) If in any action the court is satisfied that a sum less than the amount specified in subsection (1) would be equal to the loss sustained by the creditor in consequence of the termination of the agreement by the debtor, the court may make an order for the payment of that sum in lieu of the amount specified in subsection (1).

(4) If the debtor has contravened an obligation to take reasonable care of the goods or land, the amount arrived at under subsection (1) shall be increased by the sum required to recompense the creditor for that contravention, and subsection (2) shall have effect accordingly.

(5) Where the debtor, on the termination of the agreement, wrongfully retains possession of goods to which the agreement relates, then, in any action brought by the creditor to recover possession of the goods from the debtor, the court, unless it is satisfied that having regard to the circumstances it would not be just to do so, shall order the goods to be delivered to the creditor without giving the debtor an option to pay the value of the goods.

101.—(1) The hirer under a regulated consumer hire agreement is entitled to terminate the agreement by giving notice to any person entitled or authorised to receive the sums payable under the agreement.

(2) Termination of an agreement under subsection (1) does not affect any liability under the agreement which has accrued before the termination.

(3) A notice under subsection (1) shall not expire earlier than eighteen months after the making of the agreement, but apart from that the minimum period of notice to be given under subsection (1), unless the agreement provides for a shorter period, is as follows.

(4) If the agreement provides for the making of payments by the hirer to the owner at equal intervals, the minimum period of notice is the length of one interval or three months, whichever is less.

(5) If the agreement provides for the making of such payments at differing intervals, the minimum period of notice is the length of the shortest interval or three months, whichever is less.

(6) In any other case, the minimum period of notice is three months.

(7) This section does not apply to—

(a) any agreement which provides for the making by the hirer of payments which in total (and without breach of the agreement) exceed £300 in any year, or

(b) any agreement where—

(i) goods are bailed or (in Scotland) hired to the hirer for the purposes of a business carried on by him, or the hirer holds himself out as requiring the goods for those purposes, and

(ii) the goods are selected by the hirer, and acquired by the owner for the purposes of the agreement at the request of the hirer from any person other than the owner's associate, or

(c) any agreement where the hirer requires, or holds himself out as requiring, the goods for the purpose of bailing or hiring them to other persons in the course of a business carried on by him.

(8) If, on an application made to the Director by a person carrying on a consumer hire business, it appears to the Director that it would be in the interest of hirers to do so, he may by notice to the applicant direct that this section shall not apply to consumer hire agreements made by the applicant, and subject to such conditions (if any) as the Director may specify, this Act shall have effect accordingly.

(9) In the case of a modifying agreement, subsection (3) shall apply with the substitution, for " the making of the agreement " of " the making of the original agreement ".

Agency for
receiving
notice of
rescission.

102.—(1) Where the debtor or hirer under a regulated agreement claims to have a right to rescind the agreement, each of the following shall be deemed to be the agent of the creditor or owner for the purpose of receiving any notice rescinding the agreement which is served by the debtor or hirer—

(a) a credit-broker or supplier who was the negotiator in antecedent negotiations, and

(b) any person who, in the course of a business carried on by him, acted on behalf of the debtor or hirer in any negotiations for the agreement.

(2) In subsection (1) " rescind " does not include—

(a) service of a notice of cancellation, or

(b) termination of an agreement under section 99 or 101 or by the exercise of a right or power in that behalf expressly conferred by the agreement.

Termination
statements.

103.—(1) If an individual (the " customer ") serves on any person (the " trader ") a notice—

(a) stating that—

(i) the customer was the debtor or hirer under a regulated agreement described in the notice, and the trader was the creditor or owner under the agreement, and

(ii) the customer has discharged his indebtedness to the trader under the agreement, and

(iii) the agreement has ceased to have any opera-tion ; and

(b) requiring the trader to give the customer a notice, signed by or on behalf of the trader, confirming that those statements are correct,

the trader shall, within the prescribed period after receiving the notice, either comply with it or serve on the customer a counter-notice stating that, as the case may be, he disputes the correct-ness of the notice or asserts that the customer is not indebted to him under the agreement.

(2) Where the trader disputes the correctness of the notice he shall give particulars of the way in which he alleges it to be wrong.

(3) Subsection (1) does not apply in relation to any agree-ment if the trader has previously complied with that subsection on the service of a notice under it with respect to that agreement.

(4) Subsection (1) does not apply to a non-commercial agreement.

(5) If the trader fails to comply with subsection (1), and the default continues for one month, he commits an offence.

104. Goods comprised in a hire-purchase agreement or goods comprised in a conditional sale agreement which have not become vested in the debtor shall not be treated in Scotland as subject to the landlord's hypothec— *Goods not to be treated as subject to landlord's hypothec in Scotland.*

(a) during the period between the service of a default notice in respect of the goods and the date on which the notice expires or is earlier complied with ; or

(b) if the agreement is enforceable on an order of the court only, during the period between the commence-ment and termination of an action by the creditor to enforce the agreement.

PART VIII

SECURITY

General

105.—(1) Any security provided in relation to a regulated agreement shall be expressed in writing. *Form and content of securities.*

(2) Regulations may prescribe the form and content of docu-ments ("security instruments") to be made in compliance with subsection (1).

C

(3) Regulations under subsection (2) may in particular—

    (*a*) require specified information to be included in the pre-scribed manner in documents, and other specified material to be excluded ;

    (*b*) contain requirements to ensure that specified informa-tion is clearly brought to the attention of the surety, and that one part of a document is not given insuffi-cient or excessive prominence compared with another.

(4) A security instrument is not properly executed unless—

    (*a*) a document in the prescribed form, itself containing all the prescribed terms and conforming to regulations under subsection (2), is signed in the prescribed manner by or on behalf of the surety, and

    (*b*) the document embodies all the terms of the security, other than implied terms, and

    (*c*) the document, when presented or sent for the purpose of being signed by or on behalf of the surety, is in such state that its terms are readily legible, and

    (*d*) when the document is presented or sent for the pur-pose of being signed by or on behalf of the surety there is also presented or sent a copy of the document.

(5) A security instrument is not properly executed unless—

    (*a*) where the security is provided after, or at the time when, the regulated agreement is made, a copy of the executed agreement, together with a copy of any other docu-ment referred to in it, is given to the surety at the time the security is provided, or

    (*b*) where the security is provided before the regulated agreement is made, a copy of the executed agreement, together with a copy of any other document referred to in it, is given to the surety within seven days after the regulated agreement is made.

(6) Subsection (1) does not apply to a security provided by the debtor or hirer.

(7) If—

    (*a*) in contravention of subsection (1) a security is not expressed in writing, or

    (*b*) a security instrument is improperly executed,

the security, so far as provided in relation to a regulated agree-ment, is enforceable against the surety on an order of the court only.

(8) If an application for an order under subsection (7) is dis- PART VIII
missed (except on technical grounds only) section 106 (ineffective SECURITY
securities) shall apply to the security.

(9) Regulations under section 60(1) shall include provision
requiring documents embodying regulated agreements also to
embody any security provided in relation to a regulated agreement by the debtor or hirer.

106. Where, under any provision of this Act, this section is Ineffective
applied to any security provided in relation to a regulated agree- securities.
ment, then, subject to section 177 (saving for registered
charges,—

(a) the security, so far as it is so provided, shall be treated
as never having effect ;

(b) any property lodged with the creditor or owner solely
for the purposes of the security as so provided shall be
returned by him forthwith ;

(c) the creditor or owner shall take any necessary action to
remove or cancel an entry in any register, so far as the
entry relates to the security as so provided ; and

(d) any amount received by the creditor or owner on realisation of the security shall, so far as it is referable to the
agreement, be repaid to the surety.

107.—(1) The creditor under a regulated agreement for fixed- Duty to give
sum credit in relation to which security is provided, within the information to
prescribed period after receiving a request in writing to that surety under
effect from the surety and payment of a fee of 15 new pence, fixed-sum
shall give to the surety (if a different person from the debtor)— agreement.
credit

(a) a copy of the executed agreement (if any) and of any
other document referred to in it ;

(b) a copy of the security instrument (if any) ; and

(c) a statement signed by or on behalf of the creditor
showing, according to the information to which it is
practicable for him to refer,—

(i) the total sum paid under the agreement by the
debtor,

(ii) the total sum which has become payable under
the agreement by the debtor but remains unpaid, and
the various amounts comprised in that total sum,
with the date when each became due, and

(iii) the total sum which is to become payable
under the agreement by the debtor, and the various

C 2

PART VIII
SECURITY

amounts comprised in that total sum, with the date, or mode of determining the date, when each becomes due.

(2) If the creditor possesses insufficient information to enable him to ascertain the amounts and dates mentioned in subsection (1)(c)(iii), he shall be taken to comply with that sub-paragraph if his statement under subsection (1)(c) gives the basis on which, under the regulated agreement, they would fall to be ascertained.

(3) Subsection (1) does not apply to—

(a) an agreement under which no sum is, or will or may become, payable by the debtor, or

(b) a request made less than one month after a previous request under that subsection relating to the same agreement was complied with.

(4) If the creditor under an agreement fails to comply with subsection (1)—

(a) he is not entitled, while the default continues, to enforce the security, so far as provided in relation to the agreement ; and

(b) if the default continues for one month he commits an offence.

(5) This section does not apply to a non-commercial agreement.

Duty to give information to surety under running-account credit agreement.

108.—(1) The creditor under a regulated agreement for running-account credit in relation to which security is provided, within the prescribed period after receiving a request in writing to that effect from the surety and payment of a fee of 15 new pence, shall give to the surety (if a different person from the debtor)—

(a) a copy of the executed agreement (if any) and of any other document referred to in it ;

(b) a copy of the security instrument (if any) ; and

(c) a statement signed by or on behalf of the creditor showing, according to the information to which it is practicable for him to refer,—

(i) the state of the account, and

(ii) the amount, if any, currently payable under the agreement by the debtor to the creditor, and

(iii) the amounts and due dates of any payments which, if the debtor does not draw further on the account, will later become payable under the agreement by the debtor to the creditor.

(2) If the creditor possesses insufficient information to enable PART VIII
him to ascertain the amounts and dates mentioned in subsection SECURITY
(1)(*c*)(iii), he shall be taken to comply with that sub-paragraph if
his statement under subsection (1)(*c*) gives the basis on which,
under the regulated agreement, they would fall to be ascertained.

(3) Subsection (1) does not apply to—

    (*a*) an agreement under which no sum is, or will or may
become, payable by the debtor, or

    (*b*) a request made less than one month after a previous
request under that subsection relating to the same
agreement was complied with.

(4) If the creditor under an agreement fails to comply with
subsection (1)—

    (*a*) he is not entitled, while the default continues, to enforce
the security, so far as provided in relation to the
agreement ; and

    (*b*) if the default continues for one month he commits an
offence.

(5) This section does not apply to a non-commercial
agreement.

109.—(1) The owner under a regulated consumer hire agree- Duty to give
ment in relation to which security is provided, within the pre- information to
scribed period after receiving a request in writing to that effect surety under
from the surety and payment of a fee of 15 new pence, shall consumer hire
give to the surety (if a different person from the hirer)— agreement.

    (*a*) a copy of the executed agreement and of any other
document referred to in it ;

    (*b*) a copy of the security instrument (if any) ; and

    (*c*) a statement signed by or on behalf of the owner showing,
according to the information to which it is practicable
for him to refer, the total sum which has become
payable under the agreement by the hirer but remains
unpaid and the various amounts comprised in that total
sum, with the date when each became due.

(2) Subsection (1) does not apply to—

    (*a*) an agreement under which no sum is, or will or may
become, payable by the hirer, or

    (*b*) a request made less than one month after a previous
request under that subsection relating to the same
agreement was complied with.

PART VIII
SECURITY

(3) If the owner under an agreement fails to comply with subsection (1)—

(*a*) he is not entitled, while the default continues, to enforce the security, so far as provided in relation to the agreement ; and

(*b*) if the default continues for one month he commits an offence.

(4) This section does not apply to a non-commercial agreement.

Duty to give information to debtor or hirer.

110.—(1) The creditor or owner under a regulated agreement, within the prescribed period after receiving a request in writing to that effect from the debtor or hirer and payment of a fee of 15 new pence, shall give the debtor or hirer a copy of any security instrument executed in relation to the agreement after the making of the agreement.

(2) Subsection (1) does not apply to—

(*a*) a non-commercial agreement, or

(*b*) an agreement under which no sum is, or will or may become, payable by the debtor or hirer, or

(*c*) a request made less than one month after a previous request under subsection (1) relating to the same agreement was complied with.

(3) If the creditor or owner under an agreement fails to comply with subsection (1)—

(*a*) he is not entitled, while the default continues, to enforce the security (so far as provided in relation to the agreement) ; and

(*b*) if the default continues for one month he commits an offence.

Duty to give surety copy of default etc. notice.

111.—(1) When a default notice or a notice under section 76(1) or 98(1) is served on a debtor or hirer, a copy of the notice shall be served by the creditor or owner on any surety (if a different person from the debtor or hirer).

(2) If the creditor or owner fails to comply with subsection (1) in the case of any surety, the security is enforceable against the surety (in respect of the breach or other matter to which the notice relates) on an order of the court only.

Realisation of securities.

112. Subject to section 121, regulations may provide for any matters relating to the sale or other realisation, by the creditor or owner, of property over which any right has been provided by way of security in relation to an actual or prospective regulated agreement, other than a non-commercial agreement.

113.—(1) Where a security is provided in relation to an actual or prospective regulated agreement, the security shall not be enforced so as to benefit the creditor or owner, directly or indirectly, to an extent greater (whether as respects the amount of any payment or the time or manner of its being made) than would be the case if the security were not provided and any obligations of the debtor or hirer, or his relative, under or in relation to the agreement were carried out to the extent (if any) to which they would be enforced under this Act.

(2) In accordance with subsection (1), where a regulated agreement is enforceable on an order of the court or the Director only, any security provided in relation to the agreement is enforceable (so far as provided in relation to the agreement) where such an order has been made in relation to the agreement, but not otherwise.

(3) Where—

    (*a*) a regulated agreement is cancelled under section 69(1) or becomes subject to section 69(2), or

    (*b*) a regulated agreement is terminated under section 91, or

    (*c*) in relation to any agreement an application for an order under section 40(2), 65(1), 124(1) or 149(2) is dismissed (except on technical grounds only), or

    (*d*) a declaration is made by the court under section 142(1) (refusal of enforcement order) as respects any regulated agreement,

section 106 shall apply to any security provided in relation to the agreement.

(4) Where subsection (3)(*d*) applies and the declaration relates to a part only of the regulated agreement, section 106 shall apply to the security only so far as it concerns that part.

(5) In the case of a cancelled agreement, the duty imposed on the debtor or hirer by section 71 or 72 shall not be enforceable before the creditor or owner has discharged any duty imposed on him by section 106 (as applied by subsection (3)(*a*)).

(6) If the security is provided in relation to a prospective agreement or transaction, the security shall be enforceable in relation to the agreement or transaction only after the time (if any) when the agreement is made ; and until that time the person providing the security shall be entitled, by notice to the creditor or owner, to require that section 106 shall thereupon apply to the security.

(7) Where an indemnity is given in a case where the debtor or hirer is a minor, or is otherwise not of full capacity, the reference in subsection (1) to the extent to which his obligations would be enforced shall be read in relation to the indemnity as a reference to the extent to which they would be enforced if he were of full capacity.

(8) Subsections (1) to (3) also apply where a security is provided in relation to an actual or prospective linked transaction, and in that case—

(*a*) references to the agreement shall be read as references to the linked transaction, and

(*b*) references to the creditor or owner shall be read as references to any person (other than the debtor or hirer, or his relative) who is a party, or prospective party, to the linked transaction.

Pledges

Pawn-receipts.

114.—(1) At the time he receives the article, a person who takes any article in pawn under a regulated agreement shall give to the person from whom he receives it a receipt in the prescribed form (a " pawn-receipt ").

(2) A person who takes any article in pawn from an individual whom he knows to be, or who appears to be and is, a minor commits an offence.

(3) This section and sections 115 to 122 do not apply to—

(*a*) a pledge of documents of title, or

(*b*) a non-commercial agreement.

Penalty for failure to supply copies of pledge agreement, etc.

115. If the creditor under a regulated agreement to take any article in pawn fails to observe the requirements of sections 62 to 64 or 114(1) in relation to the agreement he commits an offence.

Redemption period.

116.—(1) A pawn is redeemable at any time within six months after it was taken.

(2) Subject to subsection (1), the period within which a pawn is redeemable shall be the same as the period fixed by the parties for the duration of the credit secured by the pledge, or such longer period as they may agree.

(3) If the pawn is not redeemed by the end of the period laid down by subsections (1) and (2) (the " redemption period "), it nevertheless remains redeemable until it is realised by the pawnee under section 121 except where under section 120(1)(*a*) the property in it passes to the pawnee.

(4) No special charge shall be made for redemption of a
pawn after the end of the redemption period, and charges in respect of the safe keeping of the pawn shall not be at a higher rate after the end of the redemption period than before.

117.—(1) On surrender of the pawn-receipt, and payment of the amount owing, at any time when the pawn is redeemable, the pawnee shall deliver the pawn to the bearer of the pawn-receipt.

(2) Subsection (1) does not apply if the pawnee knows or has reasonable cause to suspect that the bearer of the pawn-receipt is neither the owner of the pawn nor authorised by the owner to redeem it.

(3) The pawnee is not liable to any person in tort or delict for delivering the pawn where subsection (1) applies, or refusing to deliver it where the person demanding delivery does not comply with subsection (1) or, by reason of subsection (2), subsection (1) does not apply.

118.—(1) A person (the " claimant ") who is not in possession of the pawn-receipt but claims to be the owner of the pawn, or to be otherwise entitled or authorised to redeem it, may do so at any time when it is redeemable by tendering to the pawnee in place of the pawn-receipt—

(a) a statutory declaration made by the claimant in the prescribed form, and with the prescribed contents, or

(b) where the pawn is security for fixed-sum credit not exceeding £15 or running-account credit on which the credit limit does not exceed £15, and the pawnee agrees, a statement in writing in the prescribed form, and with the prescribed contents, signed by the claimant.

(2) On compliance by the claimant with subsection (1), section 117 shall apply as if the declaration or statement were the pawn-receipt, and the pawn-receipt itself shall become inoperative for the purposes of section 117.

119.—(1) If a person who has taken a pawn under a regu- lated agreement refuses without reasonable cause to allow the pawn to be redeemed, he commits an offence.

(2) On the conviction in England or Wales of a pawnee under subsection (1) where the offence does not amount to theft, section 28 (orders for restitution) of the Theft Act 1968, and any pro- vision of the Theft Act 1968 relating to that section, shall apply as if the pawnee had been convicted of stealing the pawn.

(3) On the conviction in Northern Ireland of a pawnee under subsection (1) where the offence does not amount to theft, section 27 (orders for restitution) of the Theft Act (Northern Ireland) 1969, and any provision of the Theft Act (Northern Ireland) 1969 relating to that section, shall apply as if the pawnee had been convicted of stealing the pawn.

Consequence
of failure
to redeem.

120.—(1) If at the end of the redemption period the pawn has not been redeemed—

(a) notwithstanding anything in section 113, the property in the pawn passes to the pawnee where the redemption period is six months and the pawn is security for fixed-sum credit not exceeding £15 or running-account credit on which the credit limit does not exceed £15 ; or

(b) in any other case the pawn becomes realisable by the pawnee.

(2) Where the debtor or hirer is entitled to apply to the court for a time order under section 129, subsection (1) shall apply with the substitution, for " at the end of the redemption period " of " after the expiry of five days following the end of the redemption period ".

Realisation
of pawn.

121.—(1) When a pawn has become realisable by him, the pawnee may sell it, after giving to the pawnor (except in such cases as may be prescribed) not less than the prescribed period of notice of the intention to sell, indicating in the notice the asking price and such other particulars as may be prescribed.

(2) Within the prescribed period after the sale takes place, the pawnee shall give the pawnor the prescribed information in writing as to the sale, its proceeds and expenses.

(3) Where the net proceeds of sale are not less than the sum which, if the pawn had been redeemed on the date of the sale, would have been payable for its redemption, the debt secured by the pawn is discharged and any surplus shall be paid by the pawnee to the pawnor.

(4) Where subsection (3) does not apply, the debt shall be treated as from the date of sale as equal to the amount by which the net proceeds of sale fall short of the sum which would have been payable for the redemption of the pawn on that date.

(5) In this section the " net proceeds of sale " is the amount realised (the " gross amount ") less the expenses (if any) of the sale.

(6) If the pawnor alleges that the gross amount is less than the true market value of the pawn on the date of sale, it is for the pawnee to prove that he and any agents employed by him in the sale used reasonable care to ensure that the true market value was obtained, and if he fails to do so subsections (3) and (4) shall have effect as if the reference in subsection (5) to the gross amount were a reference to the true market value.

(7) If the pawnor alleges that the expenses of the sale were unreasonably high, it is for the pawnee to prove that they were reasonable, and if he fails to do so subsections (3) and (4) shall have effect as if the reference in subsection (5) to expenses were a reference to reasonable expenses.

122.—(1) As respects Scotland where—
    (*a*) a pawn is either—

        (i) an article which has been stolen, or

        (ii) an article which has been obtained by fraud, and a person is convicted of any offence in relation to the theft or, as the case may be, the fraud ; or

    (*b*) a person is convicted of an offence under section 119(1),

the court by which that person is so convicted may order delivery of the pawn to the owner or the person otherwise entitled thereto.

Order in Scotland to deliver pawn.

(2) A court making an order under subsection (1)(*a*) for delivery of a pawn may make the order subject to such conditions as to payment of the debt secured by the pawn as it thinks fit.

Negotiable instruments

123.—(1) A creditor or owner shall not take a negotiable instrument, other than a bank note or cheque, in discharge of any sum payable—

Restrictions on taking and negotiating instruments.

    (*a*) by the debtor or hirer under a regulated agreement, or

    (*b*) by any person as surety in relation to the agreement.

(2) The creditor or owner shall not negotiate a cheque taken by him in discharge of a sum payable as mentioned in subsection (1) except to a banker (within the meaning of the Bills of Exchange Act 1882).

1882 c. 61.

(3) The creditor or owner shall not take a negotiable instrument as security for the discharge of any sum payable as mentioned in subsection (1).

PART VIII
SECURITY

(4) A person takes a negotiable instrument as security for the discharge of a sum if the sum is intended to be paid in some other way, and the negotiable instrument is to be presented for payment only if the sum is not paid in that way.

(5) This section does not apply where the regulated agreement is a non-commercial agreement.

(6) The Secretary of State may by order provide that this section shall not apply where the regulated agreement has a connection with a country outside the United Kingdom.

Consequences
of breach
of s. 123.

124.—(1) After any contravention of section 123 has occurred in relation to a sum payable as mentioned in section 123(1)(*a*), the agreement under which the sum is payable is enforceable against the debtor or hirer on an order of the court only.

(2) After any contravention of section 123 has occurred in relation to a sum payable by any surety, the security is enforceable on an order of the court only.

(3) Where an application for an order under subsection (2) is dismissed (except on technical grounds only) section 106 shall apply to the security.

Holders in
due course.

125.—(1) A person who takes a negotiable instrument in contravention of section 123(1) or (3) is not a holder in due course, and is not entitled to enforce the instrument.

(2) Where a person negotiates a cheque in contravention of section 123(2), his doing so constitutes a defect in his title within the meaning of the Bills of Exchange Act 1882.

1882 c. 61.

(3) If a person mentioned in section 123(1)(*a*) or (*b*) (" the protected person ") becomes liable to a holder in due course of an instrument taken from the protected person in contravention of section 123(1) or (3), or taken from the protected person and negotiated in contravention of section 123(2), the creditor or owner shall indemnify the protected person in respect of that liability.

(4) Nothing in this Act affects the rights of the holder in due course of any negotiable instrument.

Land mortgages

Enforcement
of land
mortgages.

126. A land mortgage securing a regulated agreement is enforceable (so far as provided in relation to the agreement) on an order of the court only.

PART IX

JUDICIAL CONTROL

Enforcement of certain regulated agreements and securities

127.—(1) In the case of an application for an enforcement order under—

(*a*) section 65(1) (improperly executed agreements), or

(*b*) section 105(7)(*a*) or (*b*) (improperly executed security instruments), or

(*c*) section 111(2) (failure to serve copy of notice on surety), or

(*d*) section 124(1) or (2) (taking of negotiable instrument in contravention of section 123),

the court shall dismiss the application if, but (subject to subsections (3) and (4)) only if, it considers it just to do so having regard to—

(i) prejudice caused to any person by the contravention in question, and the degree of culpability for it; and

(ii) the powers conferred on the court by subsection (2) and sections 135 and 136.

(2) If it appears to the court just to do so, it may in an enforcement order reduce or discharge any sum payable by the debtor or hirer, or any surety, so as to compensate him for prejudice suffered as a result of the contravention in question.

(3) The court shall not make an enforcement order under section 65(1) if section 61(1)(*a*) (signing of agreements) was not complied with unless a document (whether or not in the prescribed form and complying with regulations under section 60(1)) itself containing all the prescribed terms of the agreement was signed by the debtor or hirer (whether or not in the prescribed manner).

(4) The court shall not make an enforcement order under section 65(1) in the case of a cancellable agreement if—

(*a*) a provision of section 62 or 63 was not complied with, and the creditor or owner did not give a copy of the executed agreement, and of any other document referred to in it, to the debtor or hirer before the commencement of the proceedings in which the order is sought, or

(*b*) section 64(1) was not complied with.

(5) Where an enforcement order is made in a case to which subsection (3) applies, the order may direct that the regulated

Enforcement orders in cases of infringement.

agreement is to have effect as if it did not include a term omitted from the document signed by the debtor or hirer.

Enforcement
orders on
death of
debtor or
hirer.
128. The court shall make an order under section 86(2) if, but only if, the creditor or owner proves that he has been unable to satisfy himself that the present and future obligations of the debtor or hirer under the agreement are likely to be discharged.

Extension of time

Time orders.
129.—(1) If it appears to the court just to do so—

    (*a*) on an application for an enforcement order ; or

    (*b*) on an application made by a debtor or hirer under this paragraph after service on him of—

        (i) a default notice, or

        (ii) a notice under section 76(1) or 98(1) ; or

    (*c*) in an action brought by a creditor or owner to enforce a regulated agreement or any security, or recover possession of any goods or land to which a regulated agreement relates,

the court may make an order under this section (a " time order ").

(2) A time order shall provide for one or both of the following, as the court considers just—

    (*a*) the payment by the debtor or hirer or any surety of any sum owed under a regulated agreement or a security by such instalments, payable at such times, as the court, having regard to the means of the debtor or hirer and any surety, considers reasonable ;

    (*b*) the remedying by the debtor or hirer of any breach of a regulated agreement (other than non-payment of money) within such period as the court may specify.

Supplemental
provisions
about time
orders.
130.—(1) Where in accordance with rules of court an offer to pay any sum by instalments is made by the debtor or hirer and accepted by the creditor or owner, the court may in accordance with rules of court make a time order under section 129(2) (*a*) giving effect to the offer without hearing evidence of means.

(2) In the case of a hire-purchase or conditional sale agreement only, a time order under section 129(2)(*a*) may deal with sums which, although not payable by the debtor at the time the order is made, would if the agreement continued in force become payable under it subsequently.

(3) A time order under section 129(2)(*a*) shall not be made where the regulated agreement is secured by a pledge if, by virtue of regulations made under section 76(5), 87(4) or 98(5), service of a notice is not necessary for enforcement of the pledge.

(4) Where, following the making of a time order in relation PART IX
to a regulated hire-purchase or conditional sale agreement or a JUDICIAL
regulated consumer hire agreement, the debtor or hirer is in CONTROL
possession of the goods, he shall be treated (except in the case
of a debtor to whom the creditor's title has passed) as a bailee
or (in Scotland) a custodier of the goods under the terms of the
agreement, notwithstanding that the agreement has been
terminated.

(5) Without prejudice to anything done by the creditor or
owner before the commencement of the period specified in a
time order made under section 129(2)(b) ("the relevant
period "),—

(a) he shall not while the relevant period subsists take in
   relation to the agreement any action such as is
   mentioned in section 87(1) ;

(b) where—

   (i) a provision of the agreement (" the secondary
   provision ") becomes operative only on breach of
   another provision of the agreement (" the primary
   provision "), and

   (ii) the time order provides for the remedying of
   such a breach of the primary provision within the
   relevant period,

   he shall not treat the secondary provision as operative
   before the end of that period ;

(c) if while the relevant period subsists the breach to which
   the order relates is remedied it shall be treated as not
   having occurred.

(6) On the application of any person affected by a time order,
the court may vary or revoke the order.

Protection of property pending proceedings

131. The court, on the application of the creditor or owner Protection
under a regulated agreement, may make such orders as it thinks orders.
just for protecting any property of the creditor or owner, or
property subject to any security, from damage or depreciation
pending the determination of any proceedings under this Act,
including orders restricting or prohibiting use of the property
or giving directions as to its custody.

Hire and hire-purchase etc. agreements

132.—(1) Where the owner under a regulated consumer hire Financial
agreement recovers possession of goods to which the agreement relief for
relates otherwise than by action, the hirer may apply to the hirer.
court for an order that—

(a) the whole or part of any sum paid by the hirer to the
   owner in respect of the goods shall be repaid, and

(b) the obligation to pay the whole or part of any sum owed by the hirer to the owner in respect of the goods shall cease,

and if it appears to the court just to do so, having regard to the extent of the enjoyment of the goods by the hirer, the court shall grant the application in full or in part.

(2) Where in proceedings relating to a regulated consumer hire agreement the court makes an order for the delivery to the owner of goods to which the agreement relates the court may include in the order the like provision as may be made in an order under subsection (1).

Hire-purchase etc. agreements: special powers of court.

133.—(1) If, in relation to a regulated hire-purchase or conditional sale agreement, it appears to the court just to do so—

(a) on an application for an enforcement order or time order ; or

(b) in an action brought by the creditor to recover possession of goods to which the agreement relates,

the court may—

(i) make an order (a " return order ") for the return to the creditor of goods to which the agreement relates ;

(ii) make an order (a " transfer order ") for the transfer to the debtor of the creditor's title to certain goods to which the agreement relates (" the transferred goods "), and the return to the creditor of the remainder of the goods.

(2) In determining for the purposes of this section how much of the total price has been paid (" the paid-up sum "), the court may—

(a) treat any sum paid by the debtor, or owed by the creditor, in relation to the goods as part of the paid-up sum ;

(b) deduct any sum owed by the debtor in relation to the goods (otherwise than as part of the total price) from the paid-up sum,

and make corresponding reductions in amounts so owed.

(3) Where a transfer order is made, the transferred goods shall be such of the goods to which the agreement relates as the court thinks just ; but a transfer order shall be made only where the paid-up sum exceeds the part of the total price referable to the transferred goods by an amount equal to at least one-third of the unpaid balance of the total price.

(4) Notwithstanding the making of a return order or transfer order, the debtor may at any time before the goods enter the possession of the creditor, on payment of the balance of the total price and the fulfilment of any other necessary conditions, claim the goods ordered to be returned to the creditor.

(5) When, in pursuance of a time order or under this section, the total price of goods under a regulated hire-purchase agreement or regulated conditional sale agreement is paid and any other necessary conditions are fulfilled, the creditor's title to the goods vests in the debtor.

(6) If, in contravention of a return order or transfer order, any goods to which the order relates are not returned to the creditor, the court, on the application of the creditor, may—

(a) revoke so much of the order as relates to those goods, and

(b) order the debtor to pay the creditor the unpaid portion of so much of the total price as is referable to those goods.

(7) For the purposes of this section, the part of the total price referable to any goods is the part assigned to those goods by the agreement or (if no such assignment is made) the part determined by the court to be reasonable.

134.—(1) Where goods are comprised in a regulated hire- Evidence purchase agreement, regulated conditional sale agreement or of adverse regulated consumer hire agreement, and the creditor or owner— detention in hire-purchase

(a) brings an action or makes an application to enforce a etc. cases. right to recover possession of the goods from the debtor or hirer, and

(b) proves that a demand for the delivery of the goods was included in the default notice under section 88(5), or that, after the right to recover possession of the goods accrued but before the action was begun or the application was made, he made a request in writing to the debtor or hirer to surrender the goods,

then, for the purposes of the claim of the creditor or owner to recover possession of the goods, the possession of them by the debtor or hirer shall be deemed to be adverse to the creditor or owner.

(2) In subsection (1) " the debtor or hirer " includes a person in possession of the goods at any time between the debtor's or hirer's death and the grant of probate or administration, or (in Scotland) confirmation.

(3) Nothing in this section affects a claim for damages for conversion or (in Scotland) for delict.

Supplemental provisions as to orders

Power to
impose
conditions,
or suspend
operation
of order.

135.—(1) If it considers it just to do so, the court may in an order made by it in relation to a regulated agreement include provisions—

(a) making the operation of any term of the order conditional on the doing of specified acts by any party to the proceedings ;

(b) suspending the operation of any term of the order either—

(i) until such time as the court subsequently directs, or

(ii) until the occurrence of a specified act or omission.

(2) The court shall not suspend the operation of a term requiring the delivery up of goods by any person unless satisfied that the goods are in his possession or control.

(3) In the case of a consumer hire agreement, the court shall not so use its powers under subsection (1)(b) as to extend the period for which, under the terms of the agreement, the hirer is entitled to possession of the goods to which the agreement relates.

(4) On the application of any person affected by a provision included under subsection (1), the court may vary the provision.

Power to vary
agreements
and securities.

136. The court may in an order made by it under this Act include such provision as it considers just for amending any agreement or security in consequence of a term of the order.

Extortionate credit bargains

Extortionate
credit
bargains.

137.—(1) If the court finds a credit bargain extortionate it may reopen the credit agreement so as to do justice between the parties.

(2) In this section and sections 138 to 140,—

(a) " credit agreement " means any agreement between an individual (the " debtor ") and any other person (the " creditor ") by which the creditor provides the debtor with credit of any amount, and

(b) " credit bargain "—

(i) where no transaction other than the credit agreement is to be taken into account in computing the total charge for credit, means the credit agreement, or

(ii) where one or more other transactions are to
be so taken into account, means the credit agreement and those other transactions, take together.

138.—(1) A credit bargain is extortionate if it— When bargains are extortionate.

(a) requires the debtor or a relative of his to make payments (whether unconditionally, or on certain contingencies) which are grossly exorbitant, or

(b) otherwise grossly contravenes ordinary principles of fair dealing.

(2) In determining whether a credit bargain is extortionate, regard shall be had to such evidence as is adduced concerning—

(a) interest rates prevailing at the time it was made,

(b) the factors mentioned in subsection (3) to (5), and

(c) any other relevant considerations.

(3) Factors applicable under subsection (2) in relation to the debtor include—

(a) his age, experience, business capacity and state of health ; and

(b) the degree to which, at the time of making the credit bargain, he was under financial pressure, and the nature of that pressure.

(4) Factors applicable under subsection (2) in relation to the creditor include—

(a) the degree of risk accepted by him, having regard to the value of any security provided ;

(b) his relationship to the debtor ; and

(c) whether or not a colourable cash price was quoted for any goods or services included in the credit bargain.

(5) Factors applicable under subsection (2) in relation to a linked transaction include the question how far the transaction was reasonably required for the protection of debtor or creditor, or was in the interest of the debtor.

139.—(1) A credit agreement may, if the court thinks just, be Reopening of extortionate agreements.
reopened on the ground that the credit bargain is extortionate—

(a) on an application for the purpose made by the debtor or any surety to the High Court, county court or sheriff court ; or

(b) at the instance of the debtor or a surety in any proceedings to which the debtor and creditor are parties, being proceedings to enforce the credit agreement, any security relating to it, or any linked transaction ; or

(c) at the instance of the debtor or a surety in other proceedings in any court where the amount paid or payable under the credit agreement is relevant.

(2) In reopening the agreement, the court may, for the purpose of relieving the debtor or a surety from payment of any
sum in excess of that fairly due and reasonable, by order—

(a) direct accounts to be taken, or (in Scotland) an account-
ing to be made, between any persons,

(b) set aside the whole or part of any obligation imposed
on the debtor or a surety by the credit bargain or any
related agreement,

(c) require the creditor to repay the whole or part of any
sum paid under the credit bargain or any related
agreement by the debtor or a surety, whether paid to
the creditor or any other person,

(d) direct the return to the surety of any property provided
for the purposes of the security, or

(e) alter the terms of the credit agreement or any security
instrument.

(3) An order may be made under subsection (2) notwithstanding that its effect is to place a burden on the creditor in respect
of an advantage unfairly enjoyed by another person who is a
party to a linked transaction.

(4) An order under subsection (2) shall not alter the effect
of any judgment.

(5) In England and Wales an application under subsection
(1)(a) shall be brought only in the county court in the case of—

(a) a regulated agreement, or

(b) an agreement (not being a regulated agreement) under
which the creditor provides the debtor with fixed-sum
credit not exceeding £750 or running-account credit on
which the credit limit does not exceed £750.

(6) In Scotland an application under subsection (1)(a) may be
brought in the sheriff court for the district in which the debtor
or surety resides or carries on business.

(7) In Northern Ireland an application under subsection (1)(a)
may be brought in the county court in the case of—

(a) a regulated agreement, or

(b) an agreement (not being a regulated agreement) under
which the creditor provides the debtor with fixed-sum
credit not exceeding £300 or running-account credit
on which the credit limit does not exceed £300.

140. Where the credit agreement is not a regulated agreement, expressions used in sections 137 to 139 which, apart from this section, apply only to regulated agreements, shall be construed as nearly as may be as if the credit agreement were a regulated agreement.

PART IX
JUDICIAL
CONTROL
Interpretation
of sections
137 to 139.

Miscellaneous

141.—(1) In England and Wales the county court shall have jurisdiction to hear and determine—

Jurisdiction
and parties.

   (*a*) any action by the creditor or owner to enforce a regulated agreement or any security relating to it ;

   (*b*) any action to enforce any linked transaction against the debtor or hirer or his relative,

and such an action shall not be brought in any other court.

(2) Where an action or application is brought in the High Court which, by virtue of this Act, ought to have been brought in the county court it shall not be treated as improperly brought, but shall be transferred to the county court.

(3) In Scotland the sheriff court for the district in which the debtor or hirer resides or carries on business, or resided or carried on business at the date on which he last made a payment under the agreement, shall have jurisdiction to hear and determine any action falling within subsection (1) and such an action shall not be brought in any other court.

(4) In Northern Ireland the county court shall have jurisdiction to hear and determine any action or application falling within subsection (1).

(5) Except as may be provided by rules of court, all the parties to a regulated agreement, and any surety, shall be made parties to any proceedings relating to the agreement.

142.—(1) Where under any provision of this Act a thing can be done by a creditor or owner on an enforcement order only, and either—

Power to
declare rights
of parties.

   (*a*) the court dismisses (except on technical grounds only) an application for an enforcement order, or

   (*b*) where no such application has been made or such an application has been dismissed on technical grounds only, an interested party applies to the court for a declaration under this subsection,

the court may if it thinks just make a declaration that the creditor or owner is not entitled to do that thing, and thereafter no application for an enforcement order in respect of it shall be entertained.

(2) Where—

(a) a regulated agreement or linked transaction is cancelled under section 69(1), or becomes subject to section 69(2), or

(b) a regulated agreement is terminated under section 91,

and an interested party applies to the court for a declaration under this subsection, the court may make a declaration to that effect.

Northern Ireland

Jurisdiction of county court in Northern Ireland.

143. Without prejudice to any provision which may be made by rules of court made in relation to county courts in Northern Ireland such rules may provide—

(a) that any action or application such as is mentioned in section 141(4) which is brought against the debtor or hirer in the county court may be brought in the county court for the division in which the debtor or hirer resided or carried on business at the date on which he last made a payment under the regulated agreement ;

(b) that an application by a debtor or hirer or any surety under section 129(1)(b), 132(1), 139(1)(a) or 142(1)(b) which is brought in the county court may be brought in the county court for the division in which the debtor, or, as the case may be, the hirer or surety resides or carries on business ;

(c) for service of process on persons outside Northern Ireland.

Appeal from county court in Northern Ireland.

144. Any person dissatisfied—

(a) with an order, whether adverse to him or in his favour, made by a county court in Northern Ireland in the exercise of any jurisdiction conferred by this Act, or

(b) with the dismissal or refusal by such a county court of any action or application instituted by him under the provisions of this Act,

shall be entitled to appeal from the order or from the dismissal or refusal as if the order, dismissal or refusal had been made in exercise of the jurisdiction conferred by Part III of the County

1959 c. 25
(N.I.).

1964 c. 3 (N.I.).

Courts Act (Northern Ireland) 1959 and the appeal brought under the County Court Appeals Act (Northern Ireland) 1964 and sections 2 (cases stated by county court judge) and 3 (cases stated by assize judge or High Court on appeal from county court) of the last-mentioned Act shall apply accordingly.

Part X

Ancillary Credit Businesses

Definitions

145.—(1) An ancillary credit business is any business so far as Types of
ancillary
credit
business. it comprises or relates to—

   (*a*) credit brokerage,

   (*b*) debt-adjusting,

   (*c*) debt-counselling,

   (*d*) debt-collecting, or

   (*e*) the operation of a credit reference agency.

(2) Subject to section 146(5), credit brokerage is the effecting of introductions—

   (*a*) of individuals desiring to obtain credit—

      (i) to persons carrying on businesses to which this sub-paragraph applies, or

      (ii) in the case of an individual desiring to obtain credit to finance the acquisition or provision of a dwelling occupied or to be occupied by himself or his relative, to any person carrying on a business in the course of which he provides credit secured on land, or

   (*b*) of individuals desiring to obtain goods on hire to persons carrying on businesses to which this paragraph applies, or

   (*c*) of individuals desiring to obtain credit, or to obtain goods on hire, to other credit-brokers.

(3) Subsection (2)(*a*)(i) applies to—

   (*a*) a consumer credit business ;

   (*b*) a business which comprises or relates to consumer credit agreements being, otherwise than by virtue of section 16(5)(*a*), exempt agreements ;

   (*c*) a business which comprises or relates to unregulated agreements where—

      (i) the proper law of the agreement is the law of a country outside the United Kingdom, and

      (ii) if the proper law of the agreement were the law of a part of the United Kingdom it would be a regulated consumer credit agreement.

(4) Subsection (2)(*b*) applies to—

   (*a*) a consumer hire business ;

(*b*) a business which comprises or relates to unregulated agreements where—

(i) the proper law of the agreement is the law of a country outside the United Kingdom, and

(ii) if the proper law of the agreement were the law of a part of the United Kingdom it would be a regulated consumer hire agreement.

(5) Subject to section 146(6), debt-adjusting is, in relation to debts due under consumer credit agreements or consumer hire agreements,—

(*a*) negotiating with the creditor or owner, on behalf of the debtor or hirer, terms for the discharge of a debt, or

(*b*) taking over, in return for payments by the debtor or hirer, his obligation to discharge a debt, or

(*c*) any similiar activity concerned with the liquidation of a debt.

(6) Subject to section 146(6), debt-counselling is the giving of advice to debtors or hirers about the liquidation of debts due under consumer credit agreements or consumer hire agreements.

(7) Subject to section 146(6), debt-collecting is the taking of steps to procure payment of debts due under consumer credit agreements or consumer hire agreements.

(8) A credit reference agency is a person carrying on a business comprising the furnishing of persons with information relevant to the financial standing of individuals, being information collected by the agency for that purpose.

Exceptions
from section
145.

146.—(1) A barrister or advocate acting in that capacity is not to be treated as doing so in the course of any ancillary credit business.

1957 c. 27.

(2) A solicitor engaging in contentious business (as defined in section 86(1) of the Solicitors Act 1957) is not to be treated as doing so in the course of any ancillary credit business.

1933 c. 21.

(3) A solicitor within the meaning of the Solicitors (Scotland) Act 1933 engaging in business done in or for the purposes of proceedings before a court or before an arbiter is not to be treated as doing so in the course of any ancillary credit business.

1937 c. 8 (N.I.).

(4) A solicitor in Northern Ireland engaging in business done, whether as solicitor or advocate, in or for the purposes of proceedings begun before a court (including the Lands Tribunal for Northern Ireland) or before an arbitrator appointed under the Arbitration Act (Northern Ireland) 1937, not being business

contained in section 2 of the Probates and Letters of Administration Act (Ireland) 1857, is not to be treated as doing so in the course of any ancillary credit business.

(5) For the purposes of section 145(2), introductions effected by an individual by canvassing off trade premises either debtor-creditor-supplier agreements falling within section 12(a) or regulated consumer hire agreements shall be disregarded if—

(a) the introductions are not effected by him in the capacity of an employee, and

(b) he does not by any other method effect introductions falling within section 145(2).

(6) It is not debt-adjusting, debt-counselling or debt-collecting for a person to do anything in relation to a debt arising under an agreement if—

(a) he is the creditor or owner under the agreement, otherwise than by virtue of an assignment, or

(b) he is the creditor or owner under the agreement by virtue of an assignment made in connection with the transfer to the assignee of any business other than a debt-collecting business, or

(c) he is the supplier in relation to the agreement, or

(d) he is a credit-broker who has acquired the business of the person who was the supplier in relation to the agreement, or

(e) he is a person prevented by subsection (5) from being treated as a credit-broker, and the agreement was made in consequence of an introduction (whether made by him or another person) which, under subsection (5), is to be disregarded.

Licensing

147.—(1) The provisions of Part III (except section 40) apply to an ancillary credit business as they apply to a consumer credit business.

(2) Without prejudice to the generality of section 26, regulations under that section (as applied by subsection (1)) may include provisions regulating the collection and dissemination of information by credit reference agencies.

148.—(1) An agreement for the services of a person carrying on an ancillary credit business (the " trader "), if made when the trader was unlicensed, is enforceable against the other party (the " customer ") only where the Director has made an order under subsection (2) which applies to the agreement.

(2) The trader or his successor in title may apply to the Director for an order that agreements within subsection (1) are to be treated as if made when the trader was licensed.

(3) Unless the Director determines to make an order under subsection (2) in accordance with the application, he shall, before determining the application, by notice—

(a) inform the trader, giving his reasons, that, as the case may be, he is minded to refuse the application, or to grant it in terms different from those applied for, describing them, and

(b) invite the trader to submit to the Director representations in support of his application in accordance with section 34.

(4) In determining whether or not to make an order under subsection (2) in respect of any period the Director shall consider, in addition to any other relevant factors,—

(a) how far, if at all, customers under agreements made by the trader during that period were prejudiced by the trader's conduct,

(b) whether or not the Director would have been likely to grant a licence covering that period on an application by the trader, and

(c) the degree of culpability for the failure to obtain a licence.

(5) If the Director thinks fit, he may in an order under subsection (2)—

(a) limit the order to specified agreements, or agreements of a specified description or made at a specified time ;

(b) make the order conditional on the doing of specified acts by the trader.

Regulated
agreements
made on
introductions
by unlicensed
credit-broker.

149.—(1) A regulated agreement made by a debtor or hirer who, for the purpose of making that agreement, was introduced to the creditor or owner by an unlicensed credit-broker is enforceable against the debtor or hirer only where—

(a) on the application of the credit-broker, the Director has made an order under section 148(2) in respect of a period including the time when the introduction was made, and the order does not (whether in general terms or specifically) exclude the application of this paragraph to the regulated agreement, or

(b) the Director has made an order under subsection (2) which applies to the agreement.

(2) Where during any period individuals were introduced to a person carrying on a consumer credit business or consumer hire business by an unlicensed credit-broker for the purpose of making regulated agreements with the person carrying on that business, that person or his successor in title may apply to the Director for an order that regulated agreements so made are to be treated as if the credit-broker had been licensed at the time of the introduction.

PART X
ANCILLARY
CREDIT
BUSINESSES

(3) Unless the Director determines to make an order under subsection (2) in accordance with the application, he shall, before determining the application, by notice—

(a) inform the applicant, giving his reasons, that, as the case may be, he is minded to refuse the application, or to grant it in terms different from those applied for, describing them, and

(b) invite the applicant to submit to the Director representations in support of his application in accordance with section 34.

(4) In determining whether or not to make an order under subsection (2) the Director shall consider, in addition to any other relevant factors—

(a) how far, if at all, debtors or hirers under regulated agreements to which the application relates were prejudiced by the credit-broker's conduct, and

(b) the degree of culpability of the applicant in facilitating the carrying on by the credit-broker of his business when unlicensed.

(5) If the Director thinks fit, he may in an order under subsection (2)—

(a) limit the order to specified agreements, or agreements of a specified description or made at a specified time;

(b) make the order conditional on the doing of specified acts by the applicant.

150. Section 41 (as applied by section 147(1)) shall have effect as if the following entry were included in the table set out at the end—

Appeals to Secretary of State against licensing decisions.

Determination	Appellant
Refusal to make order under section 148(2) or 149(2) in accordance with terms of application.	The applicant.

PART X
ANCILLARY
CREDIT
BUSINESSES

Advertise-
ments.

Seeking business

151.—(1) Sections 44 to 47 apply to an advertisement published for the purposes of a business of credit brokerage carried on by any person, whether it advertises the services of that person or the services of persons to whom he effects introductions, as they apply to an advertisement to which Part IV applies.

(2) Sections 44, 46 and 47 apply to an advertisement, published for the purposes of a business carried on by the advertiser, indicating that he is willing to advise on debts, or engage in transactions concerned with the liquidation of debts, as they apply to an advertisement to which Part IV applies.

(3) The Secretary of State may by order provide that an advertisement published for the purposes of a business of credit brokerage, debt adjusting or debt counselling shall not fall within subsection (1) or (2) if it is of a description specified in the order.

(4) An advertisement does not fall within subsection (2) if it indicates that the advertiser is not willing to act in relation to consumer credit agreements and consumer hire agreements.

(5) In subsections (1) and (3) " credit brokerage " includes the effecting of introductions of individuals desiring to obtain credit to any person carrying on a business in the course of which he provides credit secured on land.

Application of
sections 52 to
54 to credit
brokerage etc.

152.—(1) Sections 52 to 54 apply to a business of credit brokerage, debt-adjusting or debt-counselling as they apply to a consumer credit business.

(2) In their application to a business of credit brokerage, sections 52 and 53 shall apply to the giving of quotations and information about the business of any person to whom the credit-broker effects introductions as well as to the giving of quotations and information about his own business.

Definition of
canvassing
off trade
premises
(agreements
for ancillary
credit
services).

153.—(1) An individual (the " canvasser ") canvasses off trade premises the services of a person carrying on an ancillary credit business if he solicits the entry of another individual (the " consumer ") into an agreement for the provision to the consumer of those services by making oral representations to the consumer, or any other individual, during a visit by the canvasser to any place (not excluded by subsection (2)) where the consumer, or that other individual as the case may be, is, being a visit—

    (*a*) carried out for the purpose of making such oral representations to individuals who are at that place, but

    (*b*) not carried out in response to a request made on a previous occasion.

(2) A place is excluded from subsection (1) if it is a place where (whether on a permanent or temporary basis)—

(*a*) the ancillary credit business is carried on, or

(*b*) any business is carried on by the canvasser or the person whose employee or agent the canvasser is, or by the consumer.

154. It is an offence to canvass off trade premises the services of a person carrying on a business of credit-brokerage, debt-adjusting or debt-counselling.

155.—(1) The excess over £1 of a fee or commission for his services charged by a credit-broker to an individual to whom this subsection applies shall cease to be payable or, as the case may be, shall be recoverable by the individual if the introduction does not result in his entering into a relevant agreement within the six months following the introduction (disregarding any agreement which is cancelled under section 69(1) or becomes subject to section 69(2)).

(2) Subsection (1) applies to an individual who sought an introduction for a purpose which would have been fulfilled by his entry into—

(*a*) a regulated agreement, or

(*b*) in the case of an individual such as is referred to in section 145(2)(*a*)(ii), an agreement for credit secured on land, or

(*c*) an agreement such as is referred to in section 145(3)(*b*) or (*c*) or (4)(*b*).

(3) An agreement is a relevant agreement for the purposes of subsection (1) in relation to an individual if it is an agreement such as is referred to in subsection (2) in relation to that individual.

(4) In the case of an individual desiring to obtain credit under a consumer credit agreement, any sum payable or paid by him to a credit-broker otherwise than as a fee or commission for the credit-broker's services shall for the purposes of subsection (1) be treated as such a fee or commission if it enters, or would enter, into the total charge for credit.

Entry into agreements

156. Regulations may make provision, in relation to agreements entered into in the course of a business of credit broker-age, debt-adjusting or debt-counselling, corresponding, with such

PART X
ANCILLARY
CREDIT
BUSINESSES

modifications as the Secretary of State thinks fit, to the provision which is or may be made by or under sections 55, 60, 61, 62, 63, 65, 127, 179 or 180 in relation to agreements to which those sections apply.

Credit reference agencies

Duty to
disclose
name etc.
of agency.

157.—(1) A creditor, owner or negotiator, within the prescribed period after receiving a request in writing to that effect from the debtor or hirer, shall give him notice of the name and address of any credit reference agency from which the creditor, owner or negotiator has, during the antecedent negotiations, applied for information about his financial standing.

(2) Subsection (1) does not apply to a request received more than 28 days after the termination of the antecedent negotiations, whether on the making of the regulated agreement or otherwise.

(3) If the creditor, owner or negotiator fails to comply with subsection (1) he commits an offence.

Duty of
agency to
disclose filed
information.

158.—(1) A credit reference agency, within the prescribed period after receiving,—

(*a*) a request in writing to that effect from any individual (the " consumer "), and

(*b*) such particulars as the agency may reasonably require to enable them to identify the file, and

(*c*) a fee of 25 new pence,

shall give the consumer a copy of the file relating to him kept by the agency.

(2) When giving a copy of the file under subsection (1), the agency shall also give the consumer a statement in the prescribed form of his rights under section 159.

(3) If the agency does not keep a file relating to the consumer it shall give him notice of that fact, but need not return any money paid.

(4) If the agency contravenes any provision of this section it commits an offence.

(5) In this Act " file ", in relation to an individual, means all the information about him kept by a credit reference agency, regardless of how the information is stored, and " copy of the file ", as respects information not in plain English, means a transcript reduced into plain English.

Correction
of wrong
information.

159.—(1) A consumer given information under section 158 who considers that an entry in his file is incorrect, and that if it is not corrected he is likely to be prejudiced, may give notice to the agency requiring it either to remove the entry from the file or amend it.

(2) Within 28 days after receiving a notice under subsection (1), the agency shall by notice inform the consumer that it has—

    (*a*) removed the entry from the file, or

    (*b*) amended the entry, or

    (*c*) taken no action,

and if the notice states that the agency has amended the entry it shall include a copy of the file so far as it comprises the amended entry.

(3) Within 28 days after receiving a notice under subsection (2), or where no such notice was given, within 28 days after the expiry of the period mentioned in subsection (2), the consumer may, unless he has been informed by the agency that it has removed the entry from his file, serve a further notice on the agency requiring it to add to the file an accompanying notice of correction (not exceeding 200 words) drawn up by the consumer, and include a copy of it when furnishing information included in or based on that entry.

(4) Within 28 days after receiving a notice under subsection (3), the agency, unless it intends to apply to the Director under subsection (5), shall by notice inform the consumer that it has received the notice under subsection (3) and intends to comply with it.

(5) If—

    (*a*) the consumer has not received a notice under subsection (4) within the time required, or

    (*b*) it appears to the agency that it would be improper for it to publish a notice of correction because it is incorrect, or unjustly defames any person, or is frivolous or scandalous, or is for any other reason unsuitable,

the consumer or, as the case may be, the agency may, in the prescribed manner and on payment of the specified fee, apply to the Director, who may make such order on the application as he thinks fit.

(6) If a person to whom an order under this section is directed fails to comply with it within the period specified in the order he commits an offence.

160.—(1) The Director, on an application made by a credit reference agency, may direct that this section shall apply to the agency if he is satisfied—

Alternative procedure for business consumers.

    (*a*) that compliance with section 158 in the case of consumers who carry on a business would adversely affect the service provided to its customers by the agency, and

(b) that, having regard to the methods employed by the agency and to any other relevant factors, it is probable that consumers carrying on a business would not be prejudiced by the making of the direction.

(2) Where an agency to which this section applies receives a request, particulars and a fee under section 158(1) from a consumer who carries on a business, and section 158(3) does not apply, the agency, instead of complying with section 158, may elect to deal with the matter under the following subsections.

(3) Instead of giving the consumer a copy of the file, the agency shall within the prescribed period give notice to the consumer that it is proceeding under this section, and by notice give the consumer such information included in or based on entries in the file as the Director may direct, together with a statement in the prescribed form of the consumer's rights under subsections (4) and (5).

(4) If within 28 days after receiving the information given him under subsection (3), or such longer period as the Director may allow, the consumer—

(a) gives notice to the Director that he is dissatisfied with the information, and

(b) satisfies the Director that he has taken such steps in relation to the agency as may be reasonable with a view to removing the cause of his dissatisfaction, and

(c) pays the Director the specified fee,

the Director may direct the agency to give the Director a copy of the file, and the Director may disclose to the consumer such of the information on the file as the Director thinks fit.

(5) Section 159 applies with any necessary modifications to information given to the consumer under this section as it applies to information given under section 158.

(6) If an agency making an election under subsection (2) fails to comply with subsection (3) or (4) it commits an offence.

PART XI

ENFORCEMENT OF ACT

Enforcement
authorities.

161.—(1) The following authorities (" enforcement authorities ") have a duty to enforce this Act and regulations made under it—

(a) the Director,

(b) in Great Britain, the local weights and measures authority,

(c) in Northern Ireland, the Department of Commerce for Northern Ireland.

(2) Where a local weights and measures authority in England or Wales propose to institute proceedings for an offence under this Act (other than an offence under section 162(6), 165(1) or (2) or 174(5)) it shall, as between the authority and the Director, be the duty of the authority to give the Director notice of the intended proceedings, together with a summary of the facts on which the charges are to be founded, and postpone institution of the proceedings until either—

(a) 28 days have expired since that notice was given, or

(b) the Director has notified them of receipt of the notice and summary.

(3) Every local weights and measures authority shall, whenever the Director requires, report to him in such form and with such particulars as he requires on the exercise of their functions under this Act.

(4) Where a complaint is made to the Secretary of State that all or any of the functions of a local weights and measures authority under this Act are not being properly discharged in any area, or he is of the opinion that an investigation should be made relating to the proper discharge of those functions in any area, he may cause a local inquiry to be held, and section 250(2) to (5) of the Local Government Act 1972 (evidence and costs at local inquiries), but subsection (4) (costs of department) of that section only in a case where the Secretary of State so directs, shall apply as if the inquiry were held in pursuance of section 250(1) of that Act.

1972 c. 70.

(5) The person holding an inquiry under subsection (4) shall make a written report of the results to the Secretary of State, who shall publish it together with such observations on it (if any) as he thinks fit.

(6) In the application of subsection (4) to Scotland, for the references to section 250(2) to (5) of the Local Government Act 1972, subsection (4) of that section and section 250(1) of that Act there shall be substituted respectively references to section 210(4) to (8) of the Local Government (Scotland) Act 1973, subsection (7) of that section and section 210(1) of that Act.

1972 c. 70.

1973 c. 65.

162.—(1) A duly authorised officer of an enforcement authority, at all reasonable hours and on production, if required, of his credentials, may—

Powers of entry and inspection.

(a) in order to ascertain whether a breach of any provision of or under this Act has been committed, inspect any goods and enter any premises (other than premises used only as a dwelling);

D

(*b*) if he has reasonable cause to suspect that a breach of any provision of or under this Act has been committed, in order to ascertain whether it has been committed, require any person—

    (i) carrying on, or employed in connection with, a business to produce any books or documents relating to it ; or

    (ii) having control of any information relating to a business recorded otherwise than in a legible form to provide a document containing a legible reproduction of the whole or any part of the information,

and take copies of, or of any entry in, the books or documents ;

(*c*) if he has reasonable cause to believe that a breach of any provision of or under this Act has been committed, seize and detain any goods in order to ascertain (by testing or otherwise) whether such a breach has been committed ;

(*d*) seize and detain any goods, books or documents which he has reason to believe may be required as evidence in proceedings for an offence under this Act ;

(*e*) for the purpose of exercising his powers under this subsection to seize goods, books or documents, but only if and to the extent that it is reasonably necessary for securing that the provisions of this Act and of any regulations made under it are duly observed, require any person having authority to do so to break open any container and, if that person does not comply, break it open himself.

(2) An officer seizing goods, books or documents in exercise of his powers under this section shall not do so without informing the person he seizes them from.

(3) If a justice of the peace, on sworn information in writing, or, in Scotland, a sheriff or a magistrate or justice of the peace, on evidence on oath,—

(*a*) is satisfied that there is reasonable ground to believe either—

    (i) that any goods, books or documents which a duly authorised officer has power to inspect under this section are on any premises and their inspection is likely to disclose evidence of a breach of any provision of or under this Act ; or

    (ii) that a breach of any provision of or under this Act has been, is being or is about to be committed on any premises ; and (*b*) is also satisfied either—

(i) that admission to the premises has been or is likely to be refused and that notice of intention to apply for a warrant under this subsection has been given to the occupier ; or

(ii) that an application for admission, or the giving of such a notice, would defeat the object of the entry or that the premises are unoccupied or that the occupier is temporarily absent and it might defeat the object of the entry to wait for his return,

the justice or, as the case may be, the sheriff or magistrate may by warrant under his hand, which shall continue in force for a period of one month, authorise an officer of an enforcement authority to enter the premises (by force if need be).

(4) An officer entering premises by virtue of this section may take such other persons and equipment with him as he thinks necessary ; and on leaving premises entered by virtue of a warrant under subsection (3) shall, if they are unoccupied or the occupier is temporarily absent, leave them as effectively secured against trespassers as he found them.

(5) Regulations may provide that, in cases described by the regulations, an officer of a local weights and measures authority is not to be taken to be duly authorised for the purposes of this section unless he is authorised by the Director.

(6) A person who is not a duly authorised officer of an enforcement authority, but purports to act as such under this section, commits an offence.

(7) Nothing in this section compels a barrister, advocate or solicitor to produce a document containing a privileged communication made by or to him in that capacity or authorises the seizing of any such document in his possession.

163.—(1) Where, in exercising his powers under section 162, an officer of an enforcement authority seizes and detains goods and their owner suffers loss by reason of— Compensation for loss.

(*a*) that seizure, or

(*b*) the loss, damage or deterioration of the goods during detention,

then, unless the owner is convicted of an offence under this Act committed in relation to the goods, the authority shall compensate him for the loss so suffered.

(2) Any dispute as to the right to or amount of any compensation under subsection (1) shall be determined by arbitration.

PART XI
ENFORCE-
MENT OF
ACT
Power to
make test
purchases etc.

164.—(1) An enforcement authority may—

(*a*) make, or authorise any of their officers to make on their behalf, such purchases of goods ; and

(*b*) authorise any of their officers to procure the provision of such services or facilities or to enter into such agreements or other transactions,

as may appear to them expedient for determining whether any provisions made by or under this Act are being complied with.

(2) Any act done by an officer authorised to do it under subsection (1) shall be treated for the purposes of this Act as done by him as an individual on his own behalf.

(3) Any goods seized by an officer under this Act may be tested, and in the event of such a test he shall inform the person mentioned in section 162(2) of the test results.

(4) Where any test leads to proceedings under this Act, the enforcement authority shall—

(*a*) if the goods were purchased, inform the person they were purchased from of the test results, and

(*b*) allow any person against whom the proceedings are taken to have the goods tested on his behalf if it is reasonably practicable to do so.

Obstruction
of authorised
officers.

165.—(1) Any person who—

(*a*) wilfully obstructs an officer of an enforcement authority acting in pursuance of this Act ; or

(*b*) wilfully fails to comply with any requirement properly made to him by such an officer under section 162 ; or

(*c*) without reasonable cause fails to give such an officer (so acting) other assistance or information he may reasonably require in performing his functions under this Act,

commits an offence.

(2) If any person, in giving such information as is mentioned in subsection (1)(*c*), makes any statement which he knows to be false, he commits an offence.

(3) Nothing in this section requires a person to answer any question or give any information if to do so might incriminate that person or (where that person is married) the husband or wife of that person.

Notification
of convictions
and judgments
to Director.

166.—Where a person is convicted of an offence or has a judgment given against him by or before any court in the United Kingdom and it appears to the court—

(*a*) having regard to the functions of the Director under this Act, that the conviction or judgment should be brought to the Director's attention, and (*b*) that it may not be brought to his attention unless arrangements for that purpose are made by the court, the court may make such arrangements notwithstanding that the proceedings have been finally disposed of.

167.—(1) An offence under a provision of this Act specified in column 1 of Schedule 1 is triable in the mode or modes indicated in column 3, and on conviction is punishable as indicated in column 4 (where a period of time indicates the maximum term of imprisonment, and a monetary amount indicates the maximum fine, for the offence in question).

(2) A person who contravenes any regulations made under section 44, 52, 53, or 112, or made under section 26 by virtue of section 54, commits an offence.

168.—(1) In any proceedings for an offence under this Act it is a defence for the person charged to prove—

(*a*) that his act or omission was due to a mistake, or to reliance on information supplied to him, or to an act or omission by another person, or to an accident or some other cause beyond his control, and

(*b*) that he took all reasonable precautions and exercised all due diligence to avoid such an act or omission by himself or any person under his control.

(2) If in any case the defence provided by subsection (1) involves the allegation that the act or omission was due to an act or omission by another person or to reliance on information supplied by another person, the person charged shall not, without leave of the court, be entitled to rely on that defence unless, within a period ending seven clear days before the hearing, he has served on the prosecutor a notice giving such information identifying or assisting in the identification of that other person as was then in his possession.

169. Where at any time a body corporate commits an offence under this Act with the consent or connivance of, or because of neglect by, any individual, the individual commits the like offence if at that time—

(*a*) he is a director, manager, secretary or similar officer of the body corporate, or

(*b*) he is purporting to act as such an officer, or

(*c*) the body corporate is managed by its members of whom he is one.

PART XI
ENFORCE-
MENT OF
ACT
No further
sanctions
for breach
of Act.

170.—(1) A breach of any requirement made (otherwise than by any court) by or under this Act shall incur no civil or criminal sanction as being such a breach, except to the extent (if any) expressly provided by or under this Act.

(2) In exercising his functions under this Act the Director may take account of any matter appearing to him to constitute a breach of a requirement made by or under this Act, whether or not any sanction for that breach is provided by or under this Act and, if it is so provided, whether or not proceedings have been brought in respect of the breach.

(3) Subsection (1) does not prevent the grant of an injunction, or the making of an order of certiorari, mandamus or prohibition or as respects Scotland the grant of an interdict or of an order under section 91 of the Court of Session Act 1868 (order for specific performance of statutory duty).

1868 c. 100.

Onus of proof
in various
proceedings.

171.—(1) If an agreement contains a term signifying that in the opinion of the parties section 10(3)(*b*)(iii) does not apply to the agreement, it shall be taken not to apply unless the contrary is proved.

(2) It shall be assumed in any proceedings, unless the contrary is proved, that when a person initiated a transaction as mentioned in section 19(1)(*c*) he knew the principal agreement had been made, or contemplated that it might be made.

(3) Regulations under section 44 or 52 may make provision as to the onus of proof in any proceedings to enforce the regulations.

(4) In proceedings brought by the creditor under a credit-token agreement—

    (*a*) it is for the creditor to prove that the credit-token was lawfully supplied to the debtor, and was accepted by him, and

    (*b*) if the debtor alleges that any use made of the credit-token was not authorised by him, it is for the creditor to prove either—

        (i) that the use was so authorised, or

        (ii) that the use occurred before the creditor had been given notice under section 84(3).

(5) In proceedings under section 50(1) in respect of a document received by a minor at any school or other educational establishment for minors, it is for the person sending it to him at that establishment to prove that he did not know or suspect it to be such an establishment.

(6) In proceedings under section 119(1) it is for the pawnee to prove that he had reasonable cause to refuse to allow the pawn to be redeemed.

(7) If, in proceedings referred to in section 139(1), the debtor or any surety alleges that the credit bargain is extortionate it is for the creditor to prove the contrary.

172.—(1) A statement by a creditor or owner is binding on him if given under—

    section 77(1),

    section 78(1),

    section 79(1),

    section 97(1),

    section 107(1)(*c*),

    section 108(1)(*c*), or

    section 109(1)(*c*).

(2) Where a trader—

    (*a*) gives a customer a notice in compliance with section 103(1)(*b*), or

    (*b*) gives a customer a notice under section 103(1) asserting that the customer is not indebted to him under an agreement,

the notice is binding on the trader.

(3) Where in proceedings before any court—

    (*a*) it is sought to reply on a statement or notice given as mentioned in subsection (1) or (2), and

    (*b*) the statement or notice is shown to be incorrect,

the court may direct such relief (if any) to be given to the creditor or owner from the operation of subsection (1) or (2) as appears to the court to be just.

173.—(1) A term contained in a regulated agreement or linked transaction, or in any other agreement relating to an actual or prospective regulated agreement or linked transaction, is void if, and to the extent that, it is inconsistent with a provision for the protection of the debtor or hirer or his relative or any surety contained in this Act or in any regulation made under this Act.

(2) Where a provision specifies the duty or liability of the debtor or hirer or his relative or any surety in certain circumstances, a term is inconsistent with that provision if it purports to impose, directly or indirectly, an additional duty or liability on him in those circumstances.

(3) Notwithstanding subsection (1), a provision of this Act under which a thing may be done in relation to any person on an order of the court or the Director only shall not be taken to prevent its being done at any time with that person's consent given at that time, but the refusal of such consent shall not give rise to any liability.

Part XII

Supplemental

Restrictions on disclosure of information.

174.—(1) No information obtained under or by virtue of this Act about any individual shall be disclosed without his consent.

(2) No information obtained under or by virtue of this Act about any business shall be disclosed except, so long as the business continues to be carried on, with the consent of the person for the time being carrying it on.

(3) Subsections (1) and (2) do not apply to any disclosure of information made—

1968 c. 29.

1973 c. 41.

(a) for the purpose of facilitating the performance of any functions, under this Act, the Trade Descriptions Act 1968 or Part II or III or section 125 (annual and other reports of Director) of the Fair Trading Act 1973, of the Secretary of State, any other Minister, any enforcement authority or any Northern Ireland department, or

(b) in connection with the investigation of any criminal offence or for the purposes of any criminal proceedings, or

(c) for the purposes of any civil proceedings brought under or by virtue of this Act or under Part III of the Fair Trading Act 1973.

(4) Nothing in subsections (1) and (2) shall be construed—

(a) as limiting the particulars which may be entered in the register ; or

(b) as applying to any information which has been made public as part of the register.

(5) Any person who discloses information in contravention of this section commits an offence.

Duty of persons deemed to be agents.

175. Where under this Act a person is deemed to receive a notice or payment as agent of the creditor or owner under a regulated agreement, he shall be deemed to be under a contractual duty to the creditor or owner to transmit the notice, or remit the payment, to him forthwith.

Service of documents.

176.—(1) A document to be served under this Act by one person (" the server ") on another person (" the subject ") is to be treated as properly served on the subject if dealt with as mentioned in the following subsections.

(2) The document may be delivered or sent by post to the subject, or addressed to him by name and left at his proper address.

(3) For the purposes of this Act, a document sent by post to, or left at, the address last known to the server as the address of a person shall be treated as sent by post to, or left at, his proper address.

(4) Where the document is to be served on the subject as being the person having any interest in land, and it is not practicable after reasonable inquiry to ascertain the subject's name or address, the document may be served by—

(a) addressing it to the subject by the description of the person having that interest in the land (naming it), and

(b) delivering the document to some responsible person on the land or affixing it, or a copy of it, in a conspicuous position on the land.

(5) Where a document to be served on the subject as being a debtor, hirer or surety, or as having any other capacity relevant for the purposes of this Act, is served at any time on another person who—

(a) is the person last known to the server as having that capacity, but

(b) before that time had ceased to have it,

the document shall be treated as having been served at that time on the subject.

(6) Anything done to a document in relation to a person who (whether to the knowledge of the server or not) has died shall be treated for the purposes of subsection (5) as service of the document on that person if it would have been so treated had he not died.

(7) Neither of the following enactments (which provide for the vesting of the estate of an intestate in the Probate Judge) shall be construed as authorising service on the Probate Judge of any document which is to be served under this Act—

section 9 of the Administration of Estates Act 1925 ; 1925 c. 23.

section 3 of the Administration of Estates Act (Northern Ireland) 1955. 1955 c. 24 (N.I.).

(8) References in the preceding subsections to the serving of a document on a person include the giving of the document to that person.

PART XII
SUPPLE-
MENTAL
Saving for
registered
charges.
1925 c. 21.

177.—(1) Nothing in this Act affects the rights of a proprietor of a registered charge (within the meaning of the Land Registration Act 1925), who—

> (a) became the proprietor under a transfer for valuable consideration without notice of any defect in the title arising (apart from this section) by virtue of this Act, or

> (b) derives title from such a proprietor.

1925 c. 20.

(2) Nothing in this Act affects the operation of section 104 of the Law of Property Act 1925 (protection of purchaser where mortgagee exercises power of sale).

(3) Subsection (1) does not apply to a proprietor carrying on a business of debt-collecting.

(4) Where, by virtue of subsection (1), a land mortgage is enforced which apart from this section would be treated as never having effect, the original creditor or owner shall be liable to indemnify the debtor or hirer against any loss thereby suffered by him.

(5) In the application of this section to Scotland for subsections (1) to (3) there shall be substituted the following subsections—

> " (1) Nothing in this Act affects the rights of a creditor in a heritable security who—

>> (a) became the creditor under a transfer for value without notice of any defect in the title arising (apart from this section) by virtue of this Act ; or

>> (b) derives title from such a creditor.

1924 c. 27.

1970 c. 38.

> (2) Nothing in this Act affects the operation of section 41 of the Conveyancing (Scotland) Act 1924 (protection of purchasers), or of that section as applied to standard securities by section 32 of the Conveyancing and Feudal Reform (Scotland) Act 1970.

> (3) Subsection (1) does not apply to a creditor carrying on a business of debt-collecting.".

(6) In the application of this section to Northern Ireland—

1925 c. 21.

1891 c. 66.
1970 c. 18
(N.I.).

> (a) any reference to the proprietor of a registered charge (within the meaning of the Land Registration Act 1925) shall be construed as a reference to the registered owner of a charge under the Local Registration of Title (Ireland) Act 1891 or Part IV of the Land Registration Act (Northern Ireland) 1970, and

1925 c. 20.

1881 c. 41.
1911 c. 37.

> (b) for the reference to section 104 of the Law of Property Act 1925 there shall be substituted a reference to section 21 of the Conveyancing and Law of Property Act 1881 and section 5 of the Conveyancing Act 1911.

178. The Secretary of State or the Department of Commerce for Northern Ireland may by order make such amendments or repeals of any provision of any local Act as appears to the Secretary of State or, as the case may be, the Department, necessary or expedient in consequence of the replacement by this Act of the enactments relating to pawnbrokers and money-lenders.

PART XII SUPPLE-MENTAL Local Acts.

Regulations, orders, etc.

179.—(1) Regulations may be made as to the form and content of credit-cards, trading-checks, receipts, vouchers and other documents or things issued by creditors, owners or suppliers under or in connection with regulated agreements or by other persons in connection with linked transactions, and may in particular—

Power to prescribe form etc. of secondary documents.

(a) require specified information to be included in the prescribed manner in documents, and other specified material to be excluded;

(b) contain requirements to ensure that specified information is clearly brought to the attention of the debtor or hirer, or his relative, and that one part of a document is not given insufficient or excessive prominence compared with another.

(2) If a person issues any document or thing in contravention of regulations under subsection (1) then, as from the time of the contravention but without prejudice to anything done before it, this Act shall apply as if the regulated agreement had been improperly executed by reason of a contravention of regulations under section 60(1).

180.—(1) Regulations may be made as to the form and content of documents to be issued as copies of any executed agreement, security instrument or other document referred to in this Act, and may in particular—

Power to prescribe form etc. of copies.

(a) require specified information to be included in the prescribed manner in any copy, and contain requirements to ensure that such information is clearly brought to the attention of a reader of the copy;

(b) authorise the omission from a copy of certain material contained in the original, or the inclusion of such material in condensed form.

(2) A duty imposed by any provision of this Act (except section 35) to supply a copy of any document—

(a) is not satisfied unless the copy supplied is in the prescribed form and conforms to the prescribed requirements;

(b) is not infringed by the omission of any material, or its inclusion in condensed form, if that is authorised by regulations ;

and references in this Act to copies shall be construed accordingly.

(3) Regulations may provide that a duty imposed by this Act to supply a copy of a document referred to in an unexecuted agreement or an executed agreement shall not apply to documents of a kind specified in the regulations.

Power to alter monetary limits etc.

181.—(1) The Secretary of State may by order made by statutory instrument amend, or further amend, any of the following provisions of this Act so as to reduce or increase a sum mentioned in that provision, namely, sections 8(2), 15(1)(c), 17(1), 43(3)(a), 70(6), 75(3)(b), 77(1), 78(1), 79(1), 84(1), 101(7)(a), 107(1), 108(1), 109(1), 110(1), 118(1)(b), 120(1)(a), 139(5) and (7), 155(1) and 158(1).

(2) An order under subsection (1) amending section 8(2), 15(1)(c), 17(1), 43(3)(a), 75(3)(b) or 139(5) or (7) shall be of no effect unless a draft of the order has been laid before and approved by each House of Parliament.

Regulations and orders.

182.—(1) Any power of the Secretary of State to make regulations or orders under this Act, except the power conferred by sections 2(1)(a), 181 and 192 shall be exercisable by statutory instrument subject to annulment in pursuance of a resolution of either House of Parliament.

(2) Where a power to make regulations or orders is exercisable by the Secretary of State by virtue of this Act, regulations or orders made in the exercise of that power may—

(a) make different provision in relation to different cases or classes of case, and

(b) exclude certain cases or classes of case, and

(c) contain such transitional provisions as the Secretary of State thinks fit.

(3) Regulations may provide that specified expressions, when used as described by the regulations, are to be given the prescribed meaning, notwithstanding that another meaning is intended by the person using them.

(4) Any power conferred on the Secretary of State by this Act to make orders includes power to vary or revoke an order so made.

Determina-
tions etc. by
Director.

183. The Director may vary or revoke any determination or direction made or given by him under this Act (other than Part III, or Part III as applied by section 147).

Interpretation

184.—(1) A person is an associate of an individual if that person is the individual's husband or wife, or is a relative, or the husband or wife of a relative, of the individual or of the individual's husband or wife.

(2) A person is an associate of any person with whom he is in partnership, and of the husband or wife or a relative of any individual with whom he is in partnership.

(3) A body corporate is an associate of another body corporate—

(a) if the same person is a controller of both, or a person is a controller of one and persons who are his associates, or he and persons who are his associates, are controllers of the other ; or

(b) if a group of two or more persons is a controller of each company, and the groups either consist of the same persons or could be regarded as consisting of the same persons by treating (in one or more cases) a member of either group as replaced by a person of whom he is an associate.

(4) A body corporate is an associate of another person if that person is a controller of it or if that person and persons who are his associates together are controllers of it.

(5) In this section " relative " means brother, sister, uncle, aunt, nephew, niece, lineal ancestor or lineal descendant, and references to a husband or wife include a former husband or wife and a reputed husband or wife ; and for the purposes of this subsection a relationship shall be established as if any illegitimate child, step-child or adopted child of a person had been a child born to him in wedlock.

185.—(1) Where an actual or prospective regulated agreement has two or more debtors or hirers (not being a partnership or an unincorporated body of persons)—

(a) anything required by or under this Act to be done to or in relation to the debtor or hirer shall be done to or in relation to each of them ; and

(b) anything done under this Act by or on behalf of one of them shall have effect as if done by or on behalf of all of them.

(2) Notwithstanding subsection (1)(a), where running-account credit is provided to two or more debtors jointly, any of them may by a notice signed by him (a " dispensing notice ") authorise the creditor not to comply in his case with section 78(4) (giving of periodical statement of account) ; and the dispensing notice

shall have effect accordingly until revoked by a further notice given by the debtor to the creditor:

Provided that:

(a) a dispensing notice shall not take effect if previous dispensing notices are operative in the case of the other debtor, or each of the other debtors, as the case may be ;

(b) any dispensing notices operative in relation to an agreement shall cease to have effect if any of the debtors dies.

(3) Subsection (1)(b) does not apply for the purposes of section 61(1)(a) or 127(3).

(4) Where a regulated agreement has two or more debtors or hirers (not being a partnership or an unincorporated body of persons), section 86 applies to the death of any of them.

(5) An agreement for the provision of credit, or the bailment or (in Scotland) the hiring of goods, to two or more persons jointly where—

(a) one or more of those persons is an individual, and

(b) one or more of them is a body corporate,

is a consumer credit agreement or consumer hire agreement if it would have been one had they all been individuals ; and the body corporate or bodies corporate shall accordingly be included among the debtors or hirers under the agreement.

(6) Where subsection (5) applies, references in this Act to the signing of any document by the debtor or hirer shall be construed in relation to a body corporate as referring to a signing on behalf of the body corporate.

Agreement
with more
than one
creditor or
owner.
186. Where an actual or prospective regulated agreement has two or more creditors or owners, anything required by or under this Act to be done to, or in relation to, or by, the creditor or owner shall be effective if done to, or in relation to, or by, any one of them.

Arrangements
between
creditor and
supplier.
187.—(1) A consumer credit agreement shall be treated as entered into under pre-existing arrangements between a creditor and a supplier if it is entered into in accordance with, or in furtherance of, arrangements previously made between persons mentioned in subsection (4)(a), (b) or (c).

(2) A consumer credit agreement shall be treated as entered into in contemplation of future arrangements between a creditor and a supplier if it is entered into in the expectation that arrangements will subsequently be made between persons mentioned in

subsection (4)(*a*), (*b*) or (*c*) for the supply of cash, goods and services (or any of them) to be financed by the consumer credit agreement.

(3) Arrangements shall be disregarded for the purposes of subsection (1) or (2) if—

    (*a*) they are arrangements for the making, in specified circumstances, of payments to the supplier by the creditor, and

    (*b*) the creditor holds himself out as willing to make, in such circumstances, payments of the kind to suppliers generally.

(4) The persons referred to in subsections (1) and (2) are—

    (*a*) the creditor and the supplier ;

    (*b*) one of them and an associate of the other's ;

    (*c*) an associate of one and an associate of the other's.

(5) Where the creditor is an associate of the supplier's, the consumer credit agreement shall be treated, unless the contrary is proved, as entered into under pre-existing arrangements between the creditor and the supplier.

188.—(1) Schedule 2 shall have effect for illustrating the use of terminology employed in this Act. Examples of use of new terminology.

(2) The examples given in Schedule 2 are not exhaustive.

(3) In the case of conflict between Schedule 2 and any other provision of this Act, that other provision shall prevail.

(4) The Secretary of State may by order amend Schedule 2 by adding further examples or in any other way.

189.—(1) In this Act, unless the context otherwise requires— Definitions.

    " advertisement " includes every form of advertising, whether in a publication, by television or radio, by display of notices, signs, labels, showcards or goods, by distribution of samples, circulars, catalogues, price lists or other material, by exhibition of pictures, models or films, or in any other way, and references to the publishing of advertisements shall be construed accordingly ;

    " advertiser " in relation to an advertisement, means any person indicated by the advertisement as willing to enter into transactions to which the advertisement relates ;

    " ancillary credit business " has the meaning given by section 145(1) ;

" antecedent negotiations " has the meaning given by section 56 ;

" appeal period " means the period beginning on the first day on which an appeal to the Secretary of State may be brought and ending on the last day on which it may be brought or, if it is brought, ending on its final determination, or abandonment ;

" assignment ", in relation to Scotland, means assignation ;

" associate " shall be construed in accordance with section 184 ;

1878 c. 31.
1879 c. 50.

" bill of sale " has the meaning given by section 4 of the Bills of Sale Act 1878 or, for Northern Ireland, by section 4 of the Bills of Sale (Ireland) Act 1879 ;

1962 c. 37.

" building society " has the meaning given by section 1 of the Building Societies Act 1962, and includes a Northern Ireland society as defined by section 134(4) of that Act ;

" business " includes profession or trade, and references to a business apply subject to subsection (2) ;

" cancellable agreement " means a regulated agreement which, by virtue of section 67, may be cancelled by the debtor or hirer ;

" canvass " shall be construed in accordance with sections 48 and 153 ;

" cash " includes money in any form ;

1960 c. 58.

" charity " means as respects England and Wales a charity registered under the Charities Act 1960 or an exempt charity (within the meaning of that Act), and as respects Scotland and Northern Ireland an institution or other organisation established for charitable purposes only (" organisation " including any persons administering a trust and " charitable " being construed in the same way as if it were contained in the Income Tax Acts) ;

" conditional sale agreement " means an agreement for the sale of goods or land under which the purchase price or part of it is payable by instalments, and the property in the goods or land is to remain in the seller (notwithstanding that the buyer is to be in possession of the goods or land) until such conditions as to the payment of instalments or otherwise as may be specified in the agreement are fulfilled ;

" consumer credit agreement " has the meaning given by
section 8, and includes a consumer credit agreement
which is cancelled under section 69(1), or becomes
subject to section 69(2), so far as the agreement remains
in force ;

" consumer credit business " means any business so far as
it comprises or relates to the provision of credit under
regulated consumer credit agreements ;

" consumer hire agreement " has the meaning given by
section 15 ;

" consumer hire business " means any business so far as
it comprises or relates to the bailment or (in Scotland)
the hiring of goods under regulated consumer hire
agreements ;

" controller ", in relation to a body corporate, means a
person—

(a) in accordance with whose directions or
instructions the directors of the body corporate or of
another body corporate which is its controller (or
any of them) are accustomed to act, or

(b) who, either alone or with any associate or
associates, is entitled to exercise, or control the exercise of, one third or more of the voting power at
any general meeting of the body corporate or of
another body corporate which is its controller ;

" copy " shall be construed in accordance with section 180 ;

" costs ", in relation to Scotland, means expenses ;

" court " means in relation to England and Wales the
county court, in relation to Scotland the sheriff court
and in relation to Northern Ireland the High Court or
the county court ;

" credit " shall be construed in accordance with section 9 ;

" credit-broker " means a person carrying on a business of
credit brokerage ;

" credit brokerage " has the meaning given by section 145(2) ;

" credit limit " has the meaning given by section 10(2) ;

" creditor " means the person providing credit under a
consumer credit agreement or the person to whom his
rights and duties under the agreement have passed by
assignment or operation of law, and in relation to a
prospective consumer credit agreement, includes the
prospective creditor ;

" credit reference agency " has the meaning given by section 145(8) ;

" credit-sale agreement " means an agreement for the sale of goods, under which the purchase price or part of it is payable by instalments, but which is not a conditional sale agreement ;

" credit-token " has the meaning given by section 14(1) ;

" credit-token agreement " means a regulated agreement for the provision of credit in connection with the use of a credit-token ;

" debt-adjusting " has the meaning given by section 145(5) ;

" debt-collecting " has the meaning given by section 145(7) ;

" debt-counselling " has the meaning given by section 145(6) ;

" debtor " means the individual receiving credit under a consumer credit agreement or the person to whom his rights and duties under the agreement have passed by assignment or operation of law, and in relation to a prospective consumer credit agreement includes the prospective debtor ;

" debtor-creditor agreement " has the meaning given by section 13 ;

" debtor-creditor-supplier agreement " has the meaning given by section 12 ;

" default notice " has the meaning given by section 87(1) ;

" deposit " means any sum payable by a debtor or hirer by way of deposit or down-payment, or credited or to be credited to him on account of any deposit or down-payment, whether the sum is to be or has been paid to the creditor or owner or any other person, or is to be or has been discharged by a payment of money or a transfer or delivery of goods or by any other means ;

" Director " means the Director General of Fair Trading ;

1882 c. 56.
S.I. 1972/1072
(N.I.9.).
" electric line " has the meaning given by the Electric Lighting Act 1882 or, for Northern Ireland, the Electricity Supply (Northern Ireland) Order 1972 ;

" embodies " and related words shall be construed in accordance with subsection (4) ;

" enforcement authority " has the meaning given by section 161(1) ;

" enforcement order " means an order under section 65(1), 105(7)(*a*) or (*b*), 111(2) or 124(1) or (2) ;

" executed agreement " means a document, signed by or on behalf of the parties, embodying the terms of a regulated agreement, or such of them as have been reduced to writing ;

" exempt agreement " means an agreement specified in or under section 16 ;

" finance " means to finance wholly or partly, and " financed " and " refinanced " shall be construed accordingly ;

" file " and " copy of the file " have the meanings given by section 158(5) ;

" fixed-sum credit " has the meaning given by section 10(1)(*b*) ;

" friendly society " means a society registered under the Friendly Societies Acts 1896 to 1971 or a society within the meaning of the Friendly Societies Act (Northern Ireland) 1970 ; 1970 c. 31. (N.I.).

" future arrangements " shall be construed in accordance with section 187 ;

" general notice " means a notice published by the Director at a time and in a manner appearing to him suitable for securing that the notice is seen within a reasonable time by persons likely to be affected by it ;

" give " means deliver or send by post to ;

" goods " has the meaning given by section 62(1) of the Sale of Goods Act 1893 ; 1894 c. 71. (56 & 57 Vict.).

" group licence " has the meaning given by section 22(1)(*b*) ;

" High Court " means Her Majesty's High Court of Justice, or the Court of Session in Scotland or the High Court of Justice in Northern Ireland ;

" hire-purchase agreement " means an agreement, other than a conditional sale agreement, under which—

> (*a*) goods are bailed or (in Scotland) hired in return for periodical payments by the person to whom they are bailed or hired, and

> (*b*) the property in the goods will pass to that person if the terms of the agreement are complied with and one or more of the following occurs—

>> (i) the exercise of an option to purchase by that person,

>> (ii) the doing of any other specified act by any party to the agreement,

>> (iii) the happening of any other specified event ;

" hirer " means the individual to whom goods are bailed or (in Scotland) hired under a consumer hire agreement, or the person to whom his rights and duties under the agreement have passed by assignment or operation of law, and in relation to a prospective consumer hire agreement includes the prospective hirer ;

" individual " includes a partnership or other unincorporated body of persons not consisting entirely of bodies corporate ;

" installation " means—

(a) the installing of any electric line or any gas or water pipe,

(b) the fixing of goods to the premises where they are to be used, and the alteration of premises to enable goods to be used on them,

(c) where it is reasonably necessary that goods should be constructed or erected on the premises where they are to be used, any work carried out for the purpose of constructing or erecting them on those premises ;

1958 c. 72.

1968 c. 6.
(N.I.).
" insurance company " has the meaning given by section 33(1) of the Insurance Companies Act 1958, and includes such a company as defined by section 72(1) of the Insurance Companies Act (Northern Ireland) 1968, but does not include a friendly society or an organisation of workers or organisation of employers ;

" judgment " includes an order or decree made by any court ;

" land ", includes an interest in land, and in relation to Scotland includes heritable subjects of whatever description ;

1899 c. 46.
" land improvement company " means an improvement company as defined by section 7 of the Improvement of Land Act 1899 ;

" land mortgage " includes any security charged on land ;

" licence " means a licence under Part III (including that Part as applied to ancillary credit businesses by section 147) ;

" licensed ", in relation to any act, means authorised by a licence to do the act or cause or permit another person to do it ;

" licensee ", in the case of a group licence, includes any person covered by the licence ;

" linked transaction " has the meaning given by section
19(1) ;

" local authority ", in relation to England and Wales, means
the Greater London Council, a county council, a
London borough council, a district council, the
Common Council of the City of London, or the
Council of the Isles of Scilly, and in relation to Scotland, means a regional, islands or district council, and,
in relation to Northern Ireland, means a district
council ;

" minor ", in relation to Scotland, includes pupil ;

" modifying agreement " has the meaning given by
section 82(2) ;

" mortgage ", in relation to Scotland, includes any heritable security ;

" multiple agreement " has the meaning given by section
18(1) ;

" negotiator " has the meaning given by section 56(1) ;

" non-commercial agreement " means a consumer credit
agreement or a consumer hire agreement not made by
the creditor or owner in the course of a business carried
on by him ;

" notice " means notice in writing ;

" notice of cancellation " has the meaning given by
section 69(1) ;

" owner " means a person who bails or (in Scotland) hires
out goods under a consumer hire agreement or the
person to whom his rights and duties under the agreement have passed by assignment or operation of
law, and in relation to a prospective consumer hire
agreement, includes the prospective bailor or person
from whom the goods are to be hired ;

" pawn " means any article subject to a pledge ;

" pawn-receipt " has the meaning given by section 114 ;

" pawnee " and " pawnor " include any person to whom
the rights and duties of the original pawnee or the
original pawnor, as the case may be, have passed by
assignment or operation of law ;

" payment " includes tender ;

" personal credit agreement " has the meaning given by section 8(1) ;

" pledge " means the pawnee's rights over an article taken in pawn ;

" prescribed " means prescribed by regulations made by the Secretary of State ;

" pre-existing arrangements " shall be construed in accordance with section 187 ;

" principal agreement " has the meaning given by section 19(1) ;

" protected goods " has the meaning given by section 90(7) ;

" quotation " has the meaning given by section 52(1)(*a*) ;

" redemption period " has the meaning given by section 116(3) ;

" register " means the register kept by the Director under section 35 ;

" regulated agreement " means a consumer credit agreement, or consumer hire agreement, other than an exempt agreement, and " regulated " and " unregulated " shall be construed accordingly ;

" regulations " means regulations made by the Secretary of State ;

" relative ", except in section 184, means a person who is an associate by virtue of section 184(1) ;

" representation " includes any condition or warranty, and any other statement or undertaking, whether oral or in writing ;

" restricted-use credit agreement" and "restricted-use credit" have the meanings given by section 11(1) ;

1962 c. 30.

" rules of court ", in relation to Northern Ireland means, in relation to the High Court, rules made under section 7 of the Northern Ireland Act 1962, and, in relation to any other court, rules made by the authority having for the time being power to make rules regulating the practice and procedure in that court ;

" running-account credit " shall be construed in accordance with section 10 ;

" security ", in relation to an actual or prospective consumer credit agreement or consumer hire agreement, or any linked transaction, means a mortgage, charge, pledge, bond, debenture, indemnity, guarantee, bill, note or other right provided by the debtor or hirer, or at his request (express or implied), to secure the carrying out of the obligations of the debtor or hirer under the agreement ;

" security instrument " has the meaning given by section 105(2) ;

" serve on " means deliver or send by post to ;

" signed " shall be construed in accordance with subsection (3) ;

" small agreement " has the meaning given by section 17(1), and " small " in relation to an agreement within any category shall be construed accordingly ;

" specified fee " shall be construed in accordance with section 2(4) and (5) ;

" standard licence " has the meaning given by section 22(1)(*a*) ;

" supplier " has the meaning given by section 11(1)(*b*) or 12(*c*) or 13(*c*) or, in relation to an agreement falling within section 11(1)(*a*), means the creditor, and includes a person to whom the rights and duties of a supplier (as so defined) have passed by assignment or operation of law, or (in relation to a prospective agreement) the prospective supplier ;

" surety " means the person by whom any security is provided, or the person to whom his rights and duties in relation to the security have passed by assignment or operation of law ;

" technical grounds " shall be construed in accordance with subsection (5) ;

" time order " has the meaning given by section 129(1) ;

" total charge for credit " means a sum calculated in accordance with regulations under section 20(1) ;

" total price " means the total sum payable by the debtor under a hire-purchase agreement or a conditional sale agreement, including any sum payable on the exercise of an option to purchase, but excluding any sum payable as a penalty or as compensation or damages for a breach of the agreement ;

" unexecuted agreement " means a document embodying the terms of a prospective regulated agreement, or such of them as it is intended to reduce to writing ;

" unlicensed " means without a licence, but applies only in relation to acts for which a licence is required ;

" unrestricted-use credit agreement " and " unrestricted-use credit " have the meanings given by section 11(2) ;

" working day " means any day other than—

    (a) Saturday or Sunday,

    (b) Christmas Day or Good Friday,

1971 c. 80.
    (c) a bank holiday within the meaning given by section 1 of the Banking and Financial Dealings Act 1971.

(2) A person is not to be treated as carrying on a particular type of business merely because occasionally he enters into transactions belonging to a business of that type.

(3) Any provision of this Act requiring a document to be signed is complied with by a body corporate if the document is sealed by that body.
This subsection does not apply to Scotland.

(4) A document embodies a provision if the provision is set out either in the document itself or in another document referred to in it.

(5) An application dismissed by the court or the Director shall, if the court or the Director (as the case may be) so certifies, be taken to be dismissed on technical grounds only.

(6) Except in so far as the context otherwise requires, any reference in this Act to an enactment shall be construed as a reference to that enactment as amended by or under any other enactment, including this Act.

(7) In this Act, except where otherwise indicated—

    (a) a reference to a numbered Part, section or Schedule is a reference to the Part or section of, or the Schedule to, this Act so numbered, and

    (b) a reference in a section to a numbered subsection is a reference to the subsection of that section so numbered, and

    (c) a reference in a section, subsection or Schedule to a numbered paragraph is a reference to the paragraph of that section, subsection or Schedule so numbered.

190.—(1) There shall be defrayed out of money provided by Parliament—

   (*a*) all expenses incurred by the Secretary of State in consequence of the provisions of this Act ;

   (*b*) any expenses incurred in consequence of those provisions by any other Minister of the Crown or Government department ;

   (*c*) any increase attributable to this Act in the sums payable out of money so provided under the Superannuation Act 1972 or the Fair Trading Act 1973.

(2) Any fees received by the Director under this Act shall be paid into the Consolidated Fund.

191.—(1) The Director may make arrangements with the Department of Commerce for Northern Ireland for the Department, on his behalf,—

   (*a*) to receive applications, notices and fees ;

   (*b*) to maintain, and make available for inspection and copying, copies of entries in the register ; and

   (*c*) to provide certified copies of entries in the register,

to the extent that seems to him desirable for the convenience of persons in Northern Ireland.

(2) The Director shall give general notice of any arrangements made under subsection (1).

(3) Nothing in this Act shall authorise any Northern Ireland department to incur any expenses attributable to the provisions of this Act until provision has been made for those expenses to be defrayed out of money appropriated for the purpose.

(4) The power of the Department of Commerce for Northern Ireland to make an order under section 178 shall be exercisable by statutory rule for the purposes of the Statutory Rules Act (Northern Ireland) 1958, and any such order shall be subject to negative resolution within the meaning of the Interpretation Act (Northern Ireland) 1954 as if it were a statutory instrument within the meaning of that Act.

(5) In this Act "enactment" includes an enactment of the Parliament of Northern Ireland or the Northern Ireland Assembly, and "Act" shall be construed in a corresponding manner ; and (without prejudice to section 189(6)) any reference in this Act to such an enactment shall include a reference to any enactment re-enacting it with or without modifications.

(6) Section 38 of the Interpretation Act 1889 (effect of repeals) shall have the same operation in relation to any repeal by this Act of an enactment of the Parliament of Northern Ireland as it has in relation to the repeal of an Act of the Parliament of the United Kingdom, references in that section of the Act of 1889 to Acts and enactments being construed accordingly.

Transitional
and
commence-
ment
provis:ons,
amendments
and repeals.

192.—(1) The provisions of Schedule 3 shall have effect for the purposes of this Act.

(2) The appointment of a day for the purposes of any provision of Schedule 3 shall be effected by an order of the Secretary of State made by statutory instrument; and any such order shall include a provision amending Schedule 3 so as to insert an express reference to the day appointed.

(3) Subject to subsection (4)—

> (*a*) the enactments specified in Schedule 4 shall have effect subject to the amendments specified in that Schedule (being minor amendments or amendments consequential on the preceding provisions of this Act), and

> (*b*) the enactments specified in Schedule 5 are hereby repealed to the extent shown in column 3 of that Schedule.

(4) The Secretary of State shall by order made by statutory instrument provide for the coming into operation of the amendments contained in Schedule 4 and the repeals contained in Schedule 5, and those amendments and repeals shall have effect only as provided by an order so made.

Short title
and extent.

193.—(1) This Act may be cited as the Consumer Credit Act 1974.

(2) This Act extends to Northern Ireland.

SCHEDULES

SCHEDULE 1

Section 167.

PROSECUTION AND PUNISHMENT OF OFFENCES

1 Section	2 Offence	3 Mode of prosecution	4 Imprisonment or fine
7 ...	Knowingly or recklessly giving false information to Director.	(a) Summarily. (b) On indictment.	£400. 2 years or a fine or both.
39(1) ...	Engaging in activities requiring a licence when not a licensee.	(a) Summarily (b) On indictment.	£400. 2 years or a fine or both.
39(2) ...	Carrying on a business under a name not specified in licence.	(a) Summarily. (b) On indictment.	£400. 2 years or a fine or both.
39(3) ...	Failure to notify changes in registered particulars.	(a) Summarily. (b) On indictment.	£400. 2 years or a fine or both.
45 ...	Advertising credit where goods etc. not available for cash.	(a) Summarily. (b) On indictment.	£400. 2 years or a fine or both.
46(1) ...	False or misleading advertisements.	(a) Summarily. (b) On indictment.	£400. 2 years or a fine or both.
47(1) ...	Advertising infringements.	(a) Summarily. (b) On indictment.	£400. 2 years or a fine or both.
49(1) ...	Canvassing debtor-creditor agreements off trade premises.	(a) Summarily. (b) on indictment.	£200. 1 year or a fine or both.
49(2) ...	Soliciting debtor-creditor agreements during visits made in response to previous oral requests.	(a) Summarily. (b) On indictment.	£200. 1 year or a fine or both.
50(1) ...	Sending circulars to minors.	(a) Summarily. (b) On indictment.	£400. 1 year or a fine or both.
51(1) ...	Supplying unsolicited credit-tokens.	(a) Summarily. (b) On indictment.	£400. 2 years or a fine or both.
77(4) ...	Failure of creditor under fixed-sum credit agreement to supply copies of documents etc.	Summarily.	£200.
78(6) ...	Failure of creditor under running-account credit agreement to supply copies of documents etc.	Summarily.	£200.

Sch. 1

1 Section	2 Offence	3 Mode of Prosecution	4 Imprisonment or fine
79(3)	Failure of owner under consumer hire agreement to supply copies of documents etc.	Summarily.	£200.
80(2)	Failure to tell creditor or owner whereabouts of goods.	Summarily.	£50.
85(2)	Failure of creditor to supply copy of credit-token agreement.	Summarily.	£200.
97(3)	Failure to supply debtor with statement of amount required to discharge agreement.	Summarily.	£50.
103(5)	Failure to deliver notice relating to discharge of agreements.	Summarily.	£50.
107(4)	Failure of creditor to give information to surety under fixed-sum credit agreement.	Summarily.	£200.
108(4)	Failure of creditor to give information to surety under running-account credit agreement.	Summarily.	£200.
109(3)	Failure of owner to give information to surety under consumer hire agreement.	Summarily.	£200.
110(3)	Failure of creditor or owner to supply a copy of any security instrument to debtor or hirer.	Summarily.	£200.
114(2)	Taking pledges from minors.	(*a*) Summarily.	£400.
		(*b*) On indictment.	1 year or a fine or both.
115	Failure to supply copies of a pledge agreement or pawn-receipt.	Summarily.	£200.
119(1)	Unreasonable refusal to allow pawn to be redeemed.	Summarily.	£200.
154	Canvassing ancillary credit services off trade premises.	(*a*) Summarily.	£200.
		(*b*) On indictment.	1 year or a fine or both.
157(3)	Refusal to give name etc. of credit reference agency.	Summarily.	£200.
158(4)	Failure of credit reference agency to disclose filed information.	Summarily.	£200.
159(6)	Failure of credit reference agency to correct information.	Summarily.	£200.
160(6)	Failure of credit reference agency to comply with section 160 (3) or (4).	Summarily.	£200.
162(6)	Impersonation of enforcement authority officers,	(*a*) Summarily.	£400.
		(*b*) On indictment.	2 years or a fine or both.

1 Section	2 Offence	3 Mode of prosecution	4 Imprisonment or fine
165(1)	Obstruction of enforcement authority officers.	Summarily.	£200.
165(2)	Giving false information to enforcement authority officers.	(a) Summarily.	£400.
		(b) On indictment.	2 years or a fine or both.
167(2)	Contravention of regulations under section 44, 52, 53, 54, or 112.	(a) Summarily.	£400.
		(b) On indictment.	2 years or a fine or both.
174(5)	Wrongful disclosure of information.	(a) Summarily.	£400.
		(b) On indictment.	2 years or a fine or both.

SCHEDULE 2

EXAMPLES OF USE OF NEW TERMINOLOGY

PART I

LIST OF TERMS

Term	Defined in section	Illustrated by example(s)
Advertisement	189(1)	2
Advertiser	189(1)	2
Antecedent negotiations	56	1, 2, 3, 4
Cancellable agreement	67	4
Consumer credit agreement	8	5, 6, 7, 15, 19, 21
Consumer hire agreement	15	20, 24
Credit	9	16, 19, 21
Credit-broker	189(1)	2
Credit limit	10(2)	6, 7, 19, 22, 23
Creditor	189(1)	1, 2, 3, 4
Credit-sale agreement	189(1)	5
Credit-token	14	3, 14, 16
Credit-token agreement	14	3, 14, 16, 22
Debtor-creditor agreement	13	8, 16, 17, 18
Debtor-creditor-supplier agreement ...	12	8, 16
Fixed-sum credit	10	9, 10, 17, 23
Hire-purchase agreement	189(1)	10
Individual	189(1)	19, 24
Linked transaction	19	11
Modifying agreement	82(2)	24
Multiple agreement	18	16, 18
Negotiator	56(1)	1, 2, 3, 4
Personal credit agreement	8(1)	19
Pre-existing arrangements	187	8, 21
Restricted-use credit	11	10, 12, 13, 14, 16
Running-account credit	10	15, 16, 18, 23
Small agreement	17	16, 17, 22
Supplier	189(1)	3, 14
Total charge for credit	20	5, 10
Total price...	189(1)	10
Unrestricted-use credit	11	8, 12, 16, 17, 18.

PART II

EXAMPLES

EXAMPLE 1

Facts. Correspondence passes between an employee of a money-lending company (writing on behalf of the company) and an individual about the terms on which the company would grant him a loan under a regulated agreement.

Analysis. The correspondence constitutes antecedent negotiations falling within section 56(1)(*a*), the moneylending company being both creditor and negotiator.

EXAMPLE 2

Facts. Representations are made about goods in a poster displayed by a shopkeeper near the goods, the goods being selected by a customer who has read the poster and then sold by the shopkeeper to a finance company introduced by him (with whom he has a business relationship). The goods are disposed of by the finance company to the customer under a regulated hire-purchase agreement.

Analysis. The representations in the poster constitute antecedent negotiations falling within section 56(1)(*b*), the shopkeeper being the credit-broker and negotiator and the finance company being the creditor. The poster is an advertisement and the shopkeeper is the advertiser.

EXAMPLE 3

Facts. Discussions take place between a shopkeeper and a customer about goods the customer wishes to buy using a credit-card issued by the D Bank under a regulated agreement.

Analysis. The discussions constitute antecedent negotiations falling within section 56(1)(*c*), the shopkeeper being the supplier and negotiator and the D Bank the creditor. The credit-card is a credit-token as defined in section 14(1), and the regulated agreement under which it was issued is a credit-token agreement as defined in section 14(2).

EXAMPLE 4

Facts. Discussions take place and correspondence passes between a secondhand car dealer and a customer about a car, which is then sold by the dealer to the customer under a regulated conditional sale agreement. Subsequently, on a revocation of that agreement by consent, the car is resold by the dealer to a finance company introduced by him (with whom he has a business relationship), who in turn dispose of it to the same customer under a regulated hire-purchase agreement.

Analysis. The discussions and correspondence constitute antecedent negotiations in relation both to the conditional sale agreement and the hire-purchase agreement. They fall under section 56(1)(*a*) in relation to the conditional sale agreement, the dealer being the creditor and the negotiator. In relation to the hire-purchase agreement they fall within section 56(1)(*b*), the dealer continuing to be treated as the negotiator but the finance company now being the creditor Both agreements are cancellable if the discussions took place when the individual conducting the negotiations (whether the " negotiator " or his employee or agent) was in the presence of the debtor, unless the unexecuted agreement was signed by the debtor at trade premises (as defined in section 67(*b*)) If the discussions all took place by telephone however, or the unexecuted agreement was signed by the debtor on trade premises (as so defined) the agreements are not cancellable.

EXAMPLE 5

Facts E agrees to sell to F (an individual) an item of furniture in reurn for 24 monthly instalments of £10 payable in arrear. The property in the goods passes to F immediately.

Sch. 2   *Analysis.* This is a credit-sale agreement (see definition of " credit-sale agreement " in section 189(1)). The credit provided amounts to £240 less the amount which, according to regulations made under section 20(1), constitutes the total charge for credit. (This amount is required to be deducted by section 9(4)). Accordingly the agreement falls within section 8(2) and is a consumer credit agreement.

EXAMPLE 6

Facts. The G Bank grants H (an individual) an unlimited overdraft, with an increased rate of interest on so much of any debit balance as exceeds £2,000.

Analysis. Although the overdraft purports to be unlimited, the stipulation for increased interest above £2,000 brings the agreement within section 10(3)(*b*)(ii) and it is a consumer credit agreement.

EXAMPLE 7

Facts. J is an individual who owns a small shop which usually carries a stock worth about £1,000. K makes a stocking agreement under which he undertakes to provide on short-term credit the stock needed from time to time by J without any specified limit.

Analysis. Although the agreement appears to provide unlimited credit, it is probable, having regard to the stock usually carried by J, that his indebtedness to K will not at any time rise above £5,000. Accordingly the agreement falls within section 10(3)(*b*)(iii) and is a consumer credit agreement.

EXAMPLE 8

Facts. U, a moneylender, lends £500 to V (an individual) knowing he intends to use it to buy office equipment from W. W introduced V to U, it being his practice to introduce customers needing finance to him. Sometimes U gives W a commission for this and sometimes not. U pays the £500 direct to V.

Analysis. Although this appears to fall under section 11(1)(*b*), it is excluded by section 11(3) and is therefore (by section 11(2)) an unrestricted-use credit agreement. Whether it is a debtor-creditor agreement (by section 13(*c*)) or a debtor-creditor-supplier agreement (by section 12(*c*)) depends on whether the previous dealings between U and W amount to " pre-existing arrangements ", that is whether the agreement can be taken to have been entered into " in accordance with, or in furtherance of " arrangements previously made between U and W, as laid down in section 187(1).

EXAMPLE 9

Facts. A agrees to lend B (an individual) £4,500 in nine monthly instalments of £500.

Analysis. This is a cash loan and is a form of credit (see section 9 and definition of " cash " in section 189(1)). Accordingly it falls within section 10(1)(*b*) and is fixed-sum credit amounting to £4,500.

EXAMPLE 10

Facts. C (in England) agrees to bail goods to D (an individual) in return for periodical payments. The agreement provides for the property in the goods to pass to D on payment of a total of £7,500 and the exercise by D of an option to purchase. The sum of £7,500 includes a down-payment of £1,000. It also includes an amount which, according to regulations made under section 20(1), constitutes a total charge for credit of £1,500.

Analysis. This is a hire-purchase agreement with a deposit of £1,000 and a total price of £7,500 (see definitions of " hire-purchase agreement ", " deposit " and " total price " in section 189(1)). By section 9(3), it is taken to provide credit amounting to £7,500— (£1,500 + £1,000), which equals £5,000. Under section 8(2), the agreement is therefore a consumer credit agreement, and under sections 9(3) and 11(1) it is a restricted-use credit agreement for fixed-sum credit. A similar result would follow if the agreement by C had been a hiring agreement in Scotland.

EXAMPLE 11

Facts. X (an individual) borrows £500 from Y (Finance). As a condition of the granting of the loan X is required—

   (*a*) to execute a second mortgage on his house in favour of Y (Finance), and

   (*b*) to take out a policy of insurance on his life with Y (Insurances).

In accordance with the loan agreement, the policy is charged to Y (Finance) as collateral security for the loan. The two companies are associates within the meaning of section 184(3).

Analysis. The second mortgage is a transaction for the provision of security and accordingly does not fall within section 19(1), but the taking out of the insurance policy is a linked transaction falling within section 19(1)(*a*). The charging of the policy is a separate transaction (made between different parties) for the provision of security and again is excluded from section 19(1). The only linked transaction is therefore the taking out of the insurance policy. If X had not been required by the loan agreement to take out the policy, but it had been done at the suggestion of Y (Finance) to induce them to enter into the loan agreement, it would have been a linked transaction under section 19(1)(*c*)(i) by virtue of section 19(2)(*a*).

EXAMPLE 12

Facts. The N Bank agrees to lend O (an individual) £2,000 to buy a car from P. To make sure the loan is used as intended, the N Bank stipulates that the money must be paid by it direct to P.

Analysis. The agreement is a consumer credit agreement by virtue of section 8(2). Since it falls within section 11(1)(*b*), it is a restricted-use credit agreement, P being the supplier. If the N Bank had not

E

stipulated for direct payment to the supplier, section 11(3) would have operated and made the agreement into one for unrestricted-use credit.

EXAMPLE 13

Facts. Q, a debt-adjuster, agrees to pay off debts owed by R (an individual) to various moneylenders. For this purpose the agreement provides for the making of a loan by Q to R in return for R's agreeing to repay the loan by instalments with interest. The loan money is not paid over to R but retained by Q and used to pay off the moneylenders.

Analysis. This is an agreement to refinance existing indebtedness of the debtor's, and if the loan by Q does not exceed £5,000 is a restricted-use credit agreement falling within section 11(1)(c).

EXAMPLE 14

Facts. On payment of £1, S issues to T (an individual) a trading check under which T can spend up to £20 at any shop which has agreed, or in future agrees, to accept S's trading checks.

Analysis. The trading check is a credit-token falling within section 14(1)(b). The credit-token agreement is a restricted-use credit agreement within section 11(1)(b), any shop in which the credit-token is used being the "supplier". The fact that further shops may be added after the issue of the credit-token is irrelevant in view of section 11(4).

EXAMPLE 15

Facts. A retailer L agrees with M (an individual) to open an account in M's name and, in return for M's promise to pay a specified minimum sum into the account each month and to pay a monthly charge for credit, agrees to allow to be debited to the account, in respect of purchases made by M from L, such sums as will not increase the debit balance at any time beyond the credit limit, defined in the agreement as a given multiple of the specified minimum sum.

Analysis. This agreement provides credit falling within the definition of running-account credit in section 10(1)(a). Provided the credit limit is not over £5,000, the agreement falls within section 8(2) and is a consumer credit agreement for running-account credit.

EXAMPLE 16

Facts. Under an unsecured agreement, A (Credit), an associate of the A Bank, issues to B (an individual) a credit-card for use in obtaining cash on credit from A (Credit), to be paid by branches of the A Bank (acting as agent of A (Credit)), or goods or cash from suppliers or banks who have agreed to honour credit-cards issued by A (Credit). The credit limit is £30.

Analysis. This is a credit-token agreement falling within section 14(1)(a) and (b). It is a regulated consumer credit agreement for running-account credit. Since the credit limit does not exceed £30, the agreement is a small agreement. So far as the agreement relates to goods it is a debtor-creditor-supplier agreement within section 12(*b*), since it provides restricted-use credit under section 11(1)(*b*). So far as it relates to cash it is a debtor-creditor agreement within section 13(*c*) and the credit it provides is unrestricted-use credit. This is therefore a multiple agreement. In that the whole agreement falls within several of the categories of agreement mentioned in this Act, it is, by section 18(3), to be treated as an agreement in each of those categories. So far as it is a debtor-creditor-supplier agreement providing restricted-use credit it is, by section 18(2), to be treated as a separate agreement; and similarly so far as it is a debtor-creditor agreement providing unrestricted-use credit. (See also Example 22.)

EXAMPLE 17

Facts. The manager of the C Bank agrees orally with D (an individual) to open a current account in D's name. Nothing is said about overdraft facilities. After maintaining the account in credit for some weeks, D draws a cheque in favour of E for an amount exceeding D's credit balance by £20. E presents the cheque and the Bank pay it.

Analysis. In drawing the cheque D, by implication, requests the Bank to grant him an overdraft of £20 on its usual terms as to interest and other charges. In deciding to honour the cheque, the Bank by implication accept the offer. This constitutes a regulated small consumer credit agreement for unrestricted-use, fixed-sum credit. It is a debtor-creditor agreement, and falls within section 74(1)(*b*) if covered by a determination under section 74(3). (Compare Example 18.)

EXAMPLE 18

Facts. F (an individual) has had a current account with the G Bank for many years. Although usually in credit, the account has been allowed by the Bank to become overdrawn from time to time. The maximum such overdraft has been is about £1,000. No explicit agreement has ever been made about overdraft facilities. Now, with a credit balance of £500, F draws a cheque for £1,300.

Analysis. It might well be held that the agreement with F (express or implied) under which the Bank operate his account includes an implied term giving him the right to overdraft facilities up to say £1,000. If so, the agreement is a regulated consumer credit agreement for unrestricted-use, running-account credit. It is a debtor-creditor agreement, and falls within section 74(1)(*b*) if covered by a direction under section 74(3). It is also a multiple agreement, part of which (i.e. the part not dealing with the overdraft), as referred to in section 18(1)(*a*), falls within a category of agreement not mentioned in this Act. (Compare Example 17.)

EXAMPLE 19

Facts. H (a finance house) agrees with J (a partnership of individuals) to open an unsecured loan account in J's name on which the debit balance is not to exceed £7,000 (having regard to payments

SCH. 2   into the account made from time to time by J). Interest is to be
payable in advance on this sum, with provision for yearly adjustments.
H is entitled to debit the account with interest, a " setting-up " charge,
and other charges. Before J has an opportunity to draw on the
account it is initially debited with £2,250 for advance interest and
other charges.

Analysis. This is a personal running-account credit agreement
(see sections 8(1) and 10(1)(*a*), and definition of " individual " in
section 189(1)). By section 10(2) the credit limit is £7,000. By
section 9(4) however the initial debit of £2,250, and any other charges
later debited to the account by H, are not to be treated as credit
even though time is allowed for their payment. Effect is given to
this by section 10(3). Although the credit limit of £7,000 exceeds
the amount (£5,000) specified in section 8(2) as the maximum for a
consumer credit agreement, so that the agreement is not within
section 10(3)(*a*), it is caught by section 10(3)(*b*)(i). At the beginning
J can effectively draw (as credit) no more than £4,750, so the
agreement is a consumer credit agreement.

EXAMPLE 20

Facts. K (in England) agrees with L (an individual) to bail goods
to L for a period of three years certain at £2,000 a year, payable
quarterly. The agreement contains no provision for the passing of
the property in the goods to L.

Analysis. This is not a hire-purchase agreement (see paragraph
(*b*) of the definition of that term in section 189(1)), and is capable
of subsisting for more than three months. Paragraphs (*a*) and (*b*)
of section 15(1) are therefore satisfied, but paragraph (*c*) is not.
The payments by L must exceed £5,000 if he conforms to the
agreement. It is true that under section 101 L has a right to
terminate the agreement on giving K three months' notice expiring
not earlier than eighteen months after the making of the agreement,
but that section applies only where the agreement is a regulated
consumer hire agreement apart from the section (see subsection (1)).
So the agreement is not a consumer hire agreement, though it
would be if the hire charge were say £1,500 a year, or there were
a " break " clause in it operable by either party before the hire
charges exceeded £5,000 A similar result would follow if the
agreement by K had been a hiring agreement in Scotland.

EXAMPLE 21

Facts. The P Bank decides to issue cheque cards to its customers
under a scheme whereby the bank undertakes to honour cheques of
up to £30 in every case where the payee has taken the cheque in
reliance on the cheque card, whether the customer has funds in
his account or not. The P Bank writes to the major retailers advising
them of this scheme and also publicises it by advertising. The
Bank issues a cheque card to Q (an individual), who uses it to pay
by cheque for goods costing £20 bought by Q from R, a major
retailer. At the time, Q has £500 in his account at the P Bank.

Analysis. The agreement under which the cheque card is issued to Q is a consumer credit agreement even though at all relevant times Q has more than £30 in his account. This is because Q is free to draw out his whole balance and then use the cheque card, in which case the Bank has bound itself to honour the cheque. In other words the cheque card agreement provides Q with credit, whether he avails himself of it or not. Since the amount of the credit is not subject to any express limit, the cheque card can be used any number of times. It may be presumed however that section 10(3)(*b*)(iii) will apply. The agreement is an unrestricted-use debtor-creditor agreement (by section 13(*c*)). Although the P Bank wrote to R informing R of the P Bank's willingness to honour any cheque taken by R in reliance on a cheque card, this does not constitute pre-existing arrangements as mentioned in section 13(*c*) because section 187(3) operates to prevent it. The agreement is not a credit-token agreement within section 14(1)(*b*) because payment by the P Bank to R, would be a payment of the cheque and not a payment for the goods.

Example 22

Facts. The facts are as in Example 16. On one occasion B uses the credit-card in a way which increases his debit balance with A (Credit) to £40. A (Credit) writes to B agreeing to allow the excess on that occasion only, but stating that it must be paid off within one month.

Analysis. In exceeding his credit limit B, by implication, requests A (Credit) to allow him a temporary excess (compare Example 17). A (Credit) is thus faced by B's action with the choice of treating it as a breach of contract or granting his implied request. He does the latter. If he had done the former, B would be treated as taking credit to which he was not entitled (see section 14(3)) and, subject to the terms of his contract with A (Credit), would be liable to damages for breach of contract. As it is, the agreement to allow the excess varies the original credit-token agreement by adding a new term. Under section 10(2), the new term is to be disregarded in arriving at the credit limit, so that the credit-token agreement at no time ceases to be a small agreement. By section 82(2) the later agreement is deemed to revoke the original agreement and contain provisions reproducing the combined effect of the two agreements. By section 82(4), this later agreement is exempted from Part V (except section 56).

Example 23

Facts. Under an oral agreement made on 10th January, X (an individual) has an overdraft on his current account at the Y bank with a credit limit of £100. On 15th February, when his overdraft stands at £90, X draws a cheque for £25. It is the first time that X has exceeded his credit limit, and on 16th February the bank honours the cheque.

Analysis. The agreement of 10th January is a consumer credit agreement for running-account credit. The agreement of 15th-16th February varies the earlier agreement by adding a term allowing the credit limit to be exceeded merely temporarily. By section 82(2) the later agreement is deemed to revoke the earlier agreement and reproduce the combined effect of the two agreements. By section 82(4), Part V of this Act (except section 56) does not apply to the later agreement. By section 18(5), a term allowing a merely temporary excess over the credit limit is not to be treated as a separate agreement, or as providing fixed-sum credit. The whole of the £115 owed to the bank by X on 16th February is therefore running-account credit.

EXAMPLE 24

Facts. On 1st March 1975 Z (in England) enters into an agreement with A (an unincorporated body of persons) to bail to A equipment consisting of two components (component P and component Q). The agreement is not a hire-purchase agreement and is for a fixed term of 3 years, so paragraphs (*a*) and (*b*) of section 15(1) are both satisfied. The rental is payable monthly at a rate of £2,400 a year, but the agreement provides that this is to be reduced to £1,200 a year for the remainder of the agreement if at any time during its currency A returns component Q to the owner Z. On 5th May 1976 A is incorporated as A Ltd., taking over A's assets and liabilities. On 1st March 1977, A Ltd. returns component Q. On 1st January 1978, Z and A Ltd. agree to extend the earlier agreement by one year, increasing the rental for the final year by £250 to £1,450.

Analysis. When entered into on 1st March 1975, the agreement is a consumer hire agreement. A falls within the definition of " individual " in section 189(1) and if A returns component Q before 1st May 1976 the total rental will not exceed £5,000 (see section 15(1)(*c*)). When this date is passed without component Q having been returned it is obvious that the total rental must now exceed £5,000. Does this mean that the agreement then ceases to be a consumer hire agreement? The answer is no, because there has been no change in the terms of the agreement, and without such a change the agreement cannot move from one category to the other. Similarly, the fact that A's rights and duties under the agreement pass to a body corporate on 5th May 1976 does not cause the agreement to cease to be a consumer hire agreement (see the definition of " hirer " in section 189(1)).

The effect of the modifying agreement of 1st January 1978 is governed by section 82(2), which requires it to be treated as containing provisions reproducing the combined effect of the two actual agreements, that is to say as providing that—

(*a*) obligations outstanding on 1st January 1978 are to be treated as outstanding under the modifying agreement ;

(*b*) the modifying agreement applies at the old rate of hire for the months of January and February 1978, and

(*c*) for the year beginning 1st March 1978 A Ltd. will be the bailee of component P at a rental of £1,450.

The total rental under the modifying agreement is £1,850. Accordingly the modifying agreement is a regulated agreement. Even if the total rental under the modifying agreement exceeded £5,000 it would still be regulated because of the provisions of section 82(3).

SCHEDULE 3

TRANSITIONAL AND COMMENCEMENT PROVISIONS

Note. Except as otherwise mentioned in this Schedule, the provisions of this Act come into operation on its passing, that is on 31st July 1974.

PART II OF ACT

CREDIT AGREEMENTS, HIRE AGREEMENTS AND LINKED TRANSACTIONS

Regulated agreements

1.—(1) An agreement made before the day appointed for the purposes of this paragraph is not a regulated agreement within the meaning of this Act.

(2) In this Act " prospective regulated agreement " does not include a prospective agreement which, if made as expected, would be made before the day appointed for the purposes of this paragraph.

Linked transactions

2. A transaction may be a linked transaction in relation to a regulated agreement or prospective regulated agreement even though the transaction was entered into before the day appointed for the purposes of paragraph 1.

3. Section 19(3) applies only to transactions entered into on or after the day appointed for the purposes of this paragraph.

Total charge for credit

4. Section 20 applies to consumer credit agreements whenever made.

PART III OF ACT

LICENSING OF CREDIT AND HIRE BUSINESSES

Businesses needing a licence

5.—(1) Section 21 does not apply to the carrying on of any description of consumer credit business or consumer hire business before the day appointed for the purposes of this paragraph in relation to a business of that description.

(2) Where the person carrying on any description of consumer credit business or consumer hire business applies for a licence before the day appointed for the purposes of this paragraph in relation to a business of that description, he shall be deemed to have been granted on that day a licence covering that business and continuing in force until the licence applied for is granted or, if the application is refused, until the end of the appeal period.

The register

6. Sections 35 and 36 come into operation on the day appointed for the purposes of this paragraph.

Enforcement of agreements made by unlicensed trader

7. Section 40 does not apply to a regulated agreement made in the course of any business before the day appointed for the purposes of paragraph 5 in relation to a business of that description.

PART IV OF ACT

SEEKING BUSINESS

Advertisements

8. Part IV does not apply to any advertisement published before the day appointed for the purposes of this paragraph.

Canvassing

9. Section 49 comes into operation on the day appointed for the purposes of this paragraph.

Circulars to minors

10. Section 50 comes into operation on the day appointed for the purposes of this paragraph.

Unsolicited credit-tokens

11.—(1) Section 51(1) does not apply to the giving of a credit-token before the day appointed for the purposes of this paragraph.

(2) In section 51(3), " agreement " means an agreement whenever made.

PART V OF ACT

ENTRY INTO CREDIT OR HIRE AGREEMENTS

Antecedent negotiations

12.—(1) Section 56 applies to negotiations in relation to an actual or prospective regulated agreement where the negotiations begin after the day appointed for the purposes of this paragraph.

(2) In section 56(3), " agreement ", where it first occurs, means an agreement whenever made.

General

13. Sections 57 to 59, 61 to 65 and 67 to 73 come into operation on the day appointed for the purposes of this paragraph.

14. Section 66 comes into operation on the day appointed for the purposes of this paragraph.

PART VI OF ACT

MATTERS ARISING DURING CURRENCY OF CREDIT OR HIRE AGREEMENTS

Liability of creditor for breaches by supplier

15. Section 75 comes into operation on the day appointed for the purposes of this paragraph.

Duty to give notice

16.—(1) Section 76 comes into operation on the day appointed for the purposes of this paragraph.

(2) Section 76 applies to an agreement made before the day appointed for the purposes of this paragraph where the agreement would have been a regulated agreement if made on that day.

Duty to give information

17.—(1) Sections 77 to 80 come into operation on the day appointed for the purposes of this paragraph.

(2) Sections 77 to 79 apply to an agreement made before the day appointed for the purposes of this paragraph where the agreement would have been a regulated agreement if made on that day.

Appropriation of payments

18. Section 81 comes into operation on the day appointed for the purposes of this paragraph.

Variation of agreements

19. Section 82 comes into operation on the day appointed for the purposes of this paragraph.

Misuse of credit facilities

20.—(1) Sections 83 and 84 come into operation on the day appointed for the purposes of this paragraph.

(2) Subject to sub-paragraph (4), section 83 applies to an agreement made before the day appointed for the purposes of this paragraph where the agreement would have been a regulated consumer credit agreement if made on that day.

(3) Subject to sub-paragraph (4), section 84 applies to an agreement made before the day appointed for the purposes of this paragraph where the agreement would have been a credit-token agreement if made on that day.

(4) Sections 83 and 84 do not apply to losses arising before the day appointed for the purposes of this paragraph.

(5) Section 84(4) shall be taken to be satisfied in relation to an agreement made before the day appointed for the purposes of this paragraph if, within 28 days after that day, the creditor gives notice to the debtor of the name, address and telephone number of a person stated in that notice to be the person to whom notice is to be given under section 84(3).

Duty on issue of new credit-tokens

21.—(1) Section 85 comes into operation on the day appointed for the purposes of this paragraph.

(2) Section 85 applies to an agreement made before the day appointed for the purposes of this paragraph where the agreement would have been a regulated agreement if made on that day.

F

Death of debtor or hirer

22.—(1) Section 86 comes into operation on the day appointed for the purposes of this paragraph.

(2) Section 86 applies to an agreement made before the day appointed for the purposes of this paragraph where the agreement would have been a regulated agreement if made on that day.

PART VII OF ACT

DEFAULT AND TERMINATION

Default notices

23. Sections 87 to 89 come into operation on the day appointed for the purposes of this paragraph.

Retaking of goods and land

24. Sections 90 and 91 come into operation on the day appointed for the purposes of this paragraph.

25. Section 92 comes into operation on the day appointed for the purposes of this paragraph.

Interest on default

26. Section 93 comes into operation on the day appointed for the purposes of this paragraph.

Early payment by debtor

27. Sections 94 to 97 come into operation on the day appointed for the purposes of this paragraph.

Termination of agreements

28. Section 98 comes into operation on the day appointed for the purposes of this paragraph.

29. Section 99 comes into operation on the day appointed for the purposes of this paragraph.

30. Section 100 comes into operation on the day appointed for the purposes of this paragraph.

31. Section 101 comes into operation on the day appointed for the purposes of this paragraph.

32. Section 102 comes into operation on the day appointed for the purposes of this paragraph.

33. Section 103 comes into operation on the day appointed for the purposes of this paragraph.

34. Section 104 comes into operation on the day appointed for the purposes of this paragraph.

Old agreements

35. Part VII (except sections 90, 91, 93 and 99 to 102 and 104) applies to an agreement made before the day appointed for the purposes of this paragraph where the agreement would have been a regulated agreement if made on that day.

PART VIII OF ACT

SECURITY

General

36. Section 105 comes into operation on the day appointed for the purposes of this paragraph.

37.—(1) Sections 107 to 110 come into operation on the day appointed for the purposes of this paragraph.

(2) Sections 107 to 110 apply to an agreement made before the day appointed for the purposes of this paragraph where the agreement would have been a regulated agreement if made on that day.

38.—(1) Section 111 comes into operation on the day appointed for the purposes of this paragraph.

(2) Section 111 applies to an agreement made before the day appointed for the purposes of this paragraph where the agreement would have been a regulated agreement if made on that day.

Pledges

39. Sections 114 to 122 come into operation on the day appointed for the purposes of this paragraph.

Negotiable instruments

40. Sections 123 to 125 come into operation on the day appointed for the purposes of this paragraph.

Land mortgages

41. Section 126 comes into operation on the day appointed for the purposes of this paragraph.

PART IX OF ACT

JUDICIAL CONTROL

42. Sections 137 to 140 (extortionate credit bargains) come into operation on the day appointed for the purposes of this paragraph, and apply to agreements and transactions whenever made.

43. Subject to paragraph 42, Part IX comes into operation on the day appointed for the purposes of this paragraph.

PART X OF ACT

ANCILLARY CREDIT BUSINESSES

Licensing

44.—(1) Section 21(1) does not apply (by virtue of section 147(1)) to the carrying on of any ancillary credit business before the day appointed for the purposes of this paragraph in relation to a business of that description.

(2) Where the person carrying on an ancillary credit business applies for a licence before the day appointed for the purposes of this paragraph in relation to a business of that description, he shall be deemed to have been granted on that day a licence covering that business and continuing in force until the licence applied for is granted or, if the application is refused, until the end of the appeal period.

Enforcement of agreements made by unlicensed trader

45. Section 148(1) does not apply to an agreement made in the course of any business before the day appointed for the purposes of paragraph 44 in relation to a business of that description.

Introductions by unlicensed credit-broker

46. Section 149 does not apply to a regulated agreement made on an introduction effected in the course of any business if the introduction was effected before the day appointed for the purposes of paragraph 44 in relation to a business of that description.

Advertisements

47. Subsections (1) and (2) of section 151 do not apply to any advertisement published before the day appointed for the purposes of this paragraph.

Credit reference agencies

48. Sections 157 and 158 do not apply to a request received before the day appointed for the purposes of this paragraph.

PART XII OF ACT

SUPPLEMENTAL

Interpretation

49.—(1) In the case of an agreement—

    (*a*) which was made before the day appointed for the purposes of paragraph 17, and

    (*b*) to which (by virtue of paragraph 17(2)) section 78(4) applies,

section 185(2) shall have effect as respects a notice given before that day in relation to the agreement (whether given before or after the passing of this Act) as it would have effect if section 78(4) had been in operation when the notice was given.

(2) Paragraph (1) applies to an agreement made on or after the day appointed for the purposes of paragraph 17 to provide credit on a current account opened before that day as it applies to an agreement made before that day.

50. In section 189, the definition of "local authority" shall have effect in relation to matters arising before 16th May 1975 as if for the words "regional, islands or district council" there were substituted "a county council or town council".

SCHEDULE 4   Section 192.

MINOR AND CONSEQUENTIAL AMENDMENTS

PART I

UNITED KINGDOM

Bills of Sale Act (1878) *Amendment Act* 1882   1882 c. 43.

1. The following section shall be inserted after section 7—

"Defaults under consumer credit agreements.   7A.—(1) Paragraph (1) of section 7 of this Act does not apply to a default relating to a bill of sale given by way of security for the payment of money under a regulated agreement to which section 87(1) of the Consumer Credit Act 1974 applies—

    (*a*) unless the restriction imposed by section 88(2) of that Act has ceased to apply to the bill of sale ; or

    (*b*) if, by virtue of section 89 of that Act, the default is to be treated as not having occurred.

(2) Where paragraph (1) of section 7 of this Act does apply in relation to a bill of sale such as is mentioned in subsection (1) of this section, the proviso to that section shall have effect with the substitution of "county court" for "High Court"."

Factors Act 1889   1889 c. 45.

2. At the end of section 9 insert—

"For the purposes of this section—

    (i) the buyer under a conditional sale agreement shall be deemed not to be a person who has bought or agreed to buy goods, and

    (ii) "conditional sale agreement" means an agreement for the sale of goods which is a consumer credit agreement within the meaning of the Consumer Credit Act 1974 under which the purchase price or part of it is payable by instalments, and the property in the goods is to remain in the seller (notwithstanding that the buyer is to be in possession of the goods) until such conditions as to the payment of instalments or otherwise as may be specified in the agreement are fulfilled."

Sale of Goods Act 1893

3. In section 14 (as substituted by section 3 of the Supply of Goods (Implied Terms) Act 1973) for subsection (3) substitute—

" (3) Where the seller sells goods in the course of a business and the buyer, expressly or by implication, makes known—

    (*a*) to the seller, or

    (*b*) where the purchase price or part of it is payable by instalments and the goods were previously sold by a credit-broker to the seller, to that credit-broker,

any particular purpose for which the goods are being bought, there is an implied condition that the goods supplied under the contract are reasonably fit for that purpose, whether or not that is a purpose for which such goods are commonly supplied, except where the circumstances show that the buyer does not rely, or that it is unreasonable for him to rely, on the skill or judgment of the seller or credit-broker.

In this subsection " credit-broker " means a person acting in the course of a business of credit brokerage carried on by him, that is a business of effecting introductions of individuals desiring to obtain credit—

    (i) to persons carrying on any business so far as it relates to the provision of credit, or

    (ii) to other persons engaged in credit brokerage."

4. In section 25, at the end of subsection (2) insert—

" For the purposes of this section—

    (i) the buyer under a conditional sale agreement shall be deemed not to be a person who has bought or agreed to buy goods, and

    (ii) " conditional sale agreement " means an agreement for the sale of goods which is a consumer credit agreement within the meaning of the Consumer Credit Act 1974 under which the purchase price or part of it is payable by instalments, and the property in the goods is to remain in the seller (notwithstanding that the buyer is to be in possession of the goods) until such conditions as to the payment of instalments or otherwise as may be specified in the agreement are fulfilled."

Law of Distress Amendment Act 1908

5. The following section shall be inserted after section 4—

"Hire purchase etc. agreements.   4A.—(1) Goods—

    (*a*) bailed under a hire-purchase agreement or a consumer hire agreement, or

    (*b*) agreed to be sold under a conditional sale agreement,

are, where the relevant agreement has not been terminated, excluded from the application of this Act except during the period between the service of a default notice under the Consumer Credit Act 1974 in respect of the goods and the date on which the notice expires or is earlier complied with.

SCH. 4

(2) Goods comprised in a bill of sale are excluded from the application of this Act except, during the period between service of a default notice under the Consumer Credit Act 1974 in respect of goods subject to a regulated agreement under which a bill of sale is given by way of security and the date on which the notice expires or is earlier complied with.

(3) In this section—

"conditional sale agreement" means an agreement for the sale of goods under which the purchase price or part of it is payable by instalments, and the property in the goods is to remain in the seller (notwithstanding that the buyer is to be in possession of the goods) until such conditions as to the payment of instalments or otherwise as may be specified in the agreement are fulfilled ;

"consumer hire agreement" has the meaning given by section 15 of the Consumer Credit Act 1974.

"hire-purchase agreement" means an agreement, other than a conditional sale agreement, under which—

(*a*) goods are bailed in return for periodical payments by the person to whom they are bailed, and

(*b*) the property in the goods will pass to that person if the terms of the agreement are complied with and one or more of the following occurs—

(i) the exercise of an option to purchase by that person,

(ii) the doing of any other specified act by any party to the agreement,

(iii) the happening of any other specified event ; and

"regulated agreement" has the meaning given by section 189(1) of the Consumer Credit Act 1974."

Bankruptcy Act 1914

1914 c. 59.

6. The following section shall be inserted after section 38—

" Hire purchase etc. agreement.

38A.—(1) Goods—

(*a*) bailed under a hire-purchase agreement or a consumer hire agreement, or

(*b*) agreed to be sold under a conditional sale agreement, or

SCH. 4

    (c) subject to a regulated agreement under which a bill of sale is given by way of security,

shall not be treated as the property of the bankrupt during the period between the service of a default notice under the Consumer Credit Act 1974 in respect of the goods and the date on which the notice expires or is earlier complied with.

    (2) in this section—

    " conditional sale agreement " means an agreement for the sale of goods under which the purchase price or part of it is payable by instalments, and the property in the goods is to remain in the seller (notwithstanding that the buyer is to be in possession of the goods) until such conditions as to the payment of instalments or otherwise as may be specified in the agreement are fulfilled ;

    " consumer hire agreement " has the meaning given by section 15 of the Consumer Credit Act 1974 ;

    " hire-purchase agreement " means an agreement, other than a conditional sale agreement, under which—

        (a) goods are bailed in return for periodical payments by the person to whom they are bailed, and

        (b) the property in the goods will pass to that person if the terms of the agreement are complied with and one or more of the following occurs—

            (i) the exercise of an option to purchase by that person,

            (ii) the doing of any other specified act by any party to the agreement,

            (iii) the happening of any other specified event ; and

    " regulated agreement " has the meaning given by section 189(1) of the Consumer Credit Act 1974."

1939 c. 75.

Compensation (Defence) Act 1939

    7. In section 13 after " hire-purchase agreement " insert " or a conditional sale agreement ".

    8. In section 17(1)—

    (1) After the definition of " aircraft " insert—

    " " conditional sale agreement " means an agreement for the sale of goods which is a consumer credit agreement within the meaning of the Consumer Credit Act 1974 under which the purchase price or part of it is payable by instalments, and the property in the goods is to remain in the seller (notwithstanding that the buyer is to be in possession of the goods) until such conditions as to the payment of instalments or otherwise as may be specified in the agreement are fulfilled ; ", and

(2) for the definition of " hire-purchase agreement " substitute—

" " hire-purchase agreement " means an agreement which is a consumer credit agreement within the meaning of the Consumer Credit Act 1974, other than a conditional sale agreement, under which—

   (*a*) goods are bailed or (in Scotland) hired in return for periodical payments by the person to whom they are bailed or hired, and

   (*b*) the property in the goods will pass to that person if the terms of the agreement are complied with and one or more of the following occurs—

      (i) the exercise of an option to purchase by that person,

      (ii) the doing of any other specified act by any party to the agreement,

      (iii) the happening of any other specified event ; "

Liability for War Damage (Miscellaneous Provisions) Act 1939

1939 c. 102.

9. In section 1(3), for paragraphs (*a*) and (*b*) substitute—

" (*a*) a hire-purchase agreement or a conditional sale agreement within the meaning of the Consumer Credit Act 1974 being (in either case) a consumer credit agreement as defined by that Act ; or

(*b*) a consumer hire agreement as defined by that Act."

Agriculture (Miscellaneous Provisions) Act 1950

1950 c. 17.

10. For section 1(4) substitute—

" (4) A person in possession of a machine by virtue of a hire-purchase agreement or a conditional sale agreement shall for the purposes of this section be treated as the owner of the machine.

In this subsection—

" conditional sale agreement " means an agreement for the sale of goods under which the purchase price or part of it is payable by instalments, and the property in the goods is to remain in the seller (notwithstanding that the buyer is to be in possession of the goods) until such conditions as to the payment of instalments or otherwise as may be specified in the agreement are fulfilled ; and

" hire-purchase agreement " means an agreement, other than a conditional sale agreement, under which—

   (*a*) goods are bailed or (in Scotland) hired in return for periodical payments by the person to whom they are bailed or hired, and

(*b*) the property in the goods will pass to that person if the terms of the agreement are complied with and one or more of the following occurs—

(i) the exercise of an option to purchase by that person,

(ii) the doing of any other specified act by any party to the agreement,

(iii) the happening of any other specified event."

1951 c. 63.

Rag Flock and Other Filling Materials Act 1951

11. For section 10(7) substitute—

" (7) References in this section to a sale or to selling include references to a bailment or (in Scotland) hiring under a hire-purchase agreement or to an agreement to sell under a conditional sale agreement.

In this subsection—

" conditional sale agreement " means an agreement for the sale of goods under which the purchase price or part of it is payable by instalments, and the property in the goods is to remain in the seller (notwithstanding that the buyer is to be in possession of the goods) until such conditions as to the payment of instalments or otherwise as may be specified in the agreement are fulfilled ; and

" hire-purchase agreement " means an agreement other than a conditional sale agreement, under which—

(*a*) goods are bailed or (in Scotland) hired in return for periodical payments by the person to whom they are bailed or hired, and

(*b*) the property in the goods will pass to that person if the terms of the agreement are complied with and one or more of the following occurs—

(i) the exercise of an option to purchase by that person,

(ii) the doing of any other specified act by any party to the agreement,

(iii) the happening of any other specified event."

1951 c. 65.

Reserve and Auxiliary Forces (Protection of Civil Interest) Act 1951

12. In section 4 for subsections (4), (5) and (6), substitute—

" (4) Where the appropriate court refuses leave under section 4(2) of this Act to take possession of goods subject to a hire-purchase agreement or a conditional sale agreement or to execute a judgment or order for delivery of such goods, or gives leave subject to restrictions and conditions, and the person to whom the goods are bailed, or, as the case may be, the buyer, before possession is taken or execution on the judgment or order completed, pays the total price, the creditor's title to the goods shall, notwithstanding any failure to pay the total price at the time required by the agreement, vest in that person.

(5) Where the creditor under a hire-purchase agreement or a conditional sale agreement has taken possession of the goods bailed or agreed to be sold under it, the appropriate court on an application under section 3(1)(c) of this Act, may, if it thinks fit, deal with the case as if the creditor were proceeding to take possession of the goods and, if it makes an order under that paragraph, may direct accordingly that the goods be restored to the person to whom they were bailed or, as the case may be, the buyer ; and if, after the creditor has taken possession of the goods, notice is given under that paragraph with respect to them, he shall not, so long as the notice is in force or any application in pursuance of the notice is undisposed of, deal with the goods in such a way as to prejudice the powers of the appropriate court under this subsection."

13. For section 10 substitute—

"Property in goods subject to hire-purchase agreement.

10.—(1) Where the appropriate court refuses leave under section 8(3) of this Act to take or resume possession of goods subject to a hire-purchase agreement or a conditional sale agreement or to do diligence on any decree for the delivery of such goods, or gives leave subject to restrictions and conditions, and the person to whom they are hired, or, as the case may be, the buyer before possession is taken or resumed or diligence is done, pays the total price, the creditor's title to the goods shall, notwithstanding any failure to pay the total price at the time required by the agreement, vest in that person.

(2) Where the creditor under a hire-purchase agreement or a conditional sale agreement has taken possession of the goods hired or agreed to be sold under it, the appropriate court on an application under section 9(1)(c) of this Act may, if it thinks fit, deal with the case as if the creditor were proceeding to take possession of the goods and, if it makes an order under that paragraph, may direct accordingly that the goods be restored to the person to whom they were hired or, as the case may be, the buyer ; and if, after the creditor has taken possession of the goods, notice is given under that paragraph with respect to them, he shall not, so long as the notice is in force or any application in pursuance of the notice is undisposed of, deal with the goods in such a way as to prejudice the powers of the appropriate court under this subsection ".

14. In section 64(1)—

(1) after the definition of "compulsory national service" insert—

" " conditional sale agreement " means an agreement for the sale of goods under which the purchase price or part of it is payable by instalments, and the property in the goods is to remain in the seller (notwithstanding that the buyer is to be in possession of the goods) until such conditions as to the payment of instalments or otherwise as may be specified in the agreement are fulfilled ;

" creditor " means the person by whom goods are bailed or (in Scotland) hired under a hire-purchase agreement or, as the case may be, the seller under a conditional sale agreement, or the person to whom his rights and duties have passed by assignment or operation of the law ;

" hire-purchase agreement " means an agreement, other than a conditional sale agreement, under which—

(*a*) goods are bailed or (in Scotland) hired in return for periodical payments by the person to whom they are bailed or hired, and

(*b*) the property in the goods will pass to that person if the terms of the agreement are complied with and one or more of the following occurs—

    (i) the exercise of an option to purchase by that person,

    (ii) the doing of any other specified act by any party to the agreement,

    (iii) the happening of any other specified event ; ".

(2) After the definition of " short period of training " insert—

" " total price " means the total sum payable by the person to whom goods are bailed or hired under a hire-purchase agreement or, as the case may be, the buyer under a conditional sale agreement including any sum payable on the exercise of an option to purchase but excluding any sum payable as a penalty or as compensation or damages for a breach of the agreement ".

Clean Air Act 1956

15. In section 14 for the words " a hire-purchase agreement for the letting to him " substitute—

" either—

    (i) a conditional sale agreement for the sale to him, or

    (ii) a hire-purchase agreement for the bailment or (in Scotland) hiring to him,".

16. In section 34(1)—

(*a*) after the definition of " chimney " insert—

" " conditional sale agreement " means an agreement for the sale of goods under which the purchase price or part of it is payable by instalments, and the property in the goods is to remain in the seller (notwithstanding that the buyer is to be in possession of the goods) until such conditions as to the payment of instalments or otherwise as may be specified in the agreement are fulfilled ; ", and (*b*) for the definition of " hire-purchase agreement " substitute— Sᴄʜ. 4

" hire-purchase agreement " means an agreement, other than a conditional sale agreement under which—

(*a*) goods are bailed or (in Scotland) hired in return for periodical payments by the person to whom they are bailed or hired, and

(*b*) the property in the goods will pass to that person if the terms of the agreement are complied with and one or more of the following occurs—

(i) the exercise of an option to purchase by that person,

(ii) the doing of any other specified act by any party to the agreement,

(iii) the happening of any other specified event ; ".

Restrictive Trade Practices Act 1956

1956 c. 68.

17. For section 26(3) substitute—

" (3) In this Part of this Act any reference to selling goods includes a reference to bailing or (in Scotland) hiring goods under a hire-purchase agreement or to agreeing to sell the goods under a conditional sale agreement.

In this subsection—

(1) " conditional sale agreement " means an agreement for the sale of goods under which the purchase price or part of it is payable by instalments, and the property in the goods is to remain in the seller (notwithstanding that the buyer is to be in possession of the goods) until such conditions as to the payment of instalments or otherwise as may be specified in the agreement are fulfilled ; and

(2) " hire-purchase agreement " means an agreement, other than a conditional sale agreement, under which—

(*a*) goods are bailed or (in Scotland) hired in return for periodical payments by the person to whom they are bailed or hired, and

(*b*) the property in the goods will pass to that person if the terms of the agreement are complied with and one or more of the following occurs—

(i) the exercise of an option to purchase by that person,

(ii) the doing of any other specified act by any party to the agreement,

(iii) the happening of any other specified event."

Housing Act 1957

1957 c. 56.

18. For section 94 substitute—

"Power to provide furniture.

94. A local authority may fit out, furnish and supply any house erected, converted or acquired by them under section 92 of this Act with all requisite furniture, fittings

and conveniences and may sell, or supply under a hire-purchase agreement or a conditional sale agreement, furniture to the occupants of houses provided by the local authority and, for that purpose may buy furniture.

In this subsection—

(1) " conditional sale agreement " means an agreement for the sale of goods under which the purchase price or part of it is payable by instalments, and the property in the goods is to remain in the seller (notwithstanding that the buyer is to be in possession of the goods) until such conditions as to the payment of instalments or otherwise as may be specified in the agreement are fulfilled ; and

(2) " hire-purchase agreement " means an agreement, other than a conditional sale agreement, under which—

(a) goods are bailed in return for periodical payments by the person to whom they are bailed, and

(b) the property in the goods will pass to that person if the terms of the agreement are complied with and one or more of the following occurs—

(i) the exercise of an option to purchase by that person,

(ii) the doing of any other specified act by any party to the agreement,

(iii) the happening of any other specified event."

County Courts Act 1959

19. At the end of section 192(2)(c) insert—

" (d) section 139(5)(b) of the Consumer Credit Act 1974."

Consumer Protection Act 1961

20. In section 2, for subsection (6) substitute—

" (6) If as respects goods of any class or description regulations under section 1 above so provide, subsections (1) to (3) above (other than subsection 3(d) and (e)) shall apply in relation to goods of that class or description as if—

(a) references to selling or to a sale included references to—

(i) bailing or (in Scotland) hiring under a hire-purchase agreement, or

(ii) bailing or (in Scotland) hiring under a hire agreement, or

(iii) an agreement to sell under a conditional sale agreement ; and

(*b*) the reference to a sale under a credit-sale agreement
were a reference

(i) to a bailment, or a hiring under a hire-purchase
agreement, or

(ii) to àn agreement to sell under a conditional
sale agreement.

Provided that subsections (1) and (2) above shall not apply—

(*a*) in a case of bailment or hiring under a hire agreement,
where the bailment or hiring is incidental to an agreement under which payments are to be made in the
form of rent issuing out of land ;

(*b*) in a case of possession for the purpose of bailment or
hiring under a hire agreement, where possession is for
the purpose of a bailment or hiring which is incidental
to an agreement under which payments are to be made
in the form of rent issuing out of land ;

(*c*) in any case of bailment or hire under a hire agreement,
where the bailment or hiring was lawful at the time
when it began."

21. In section 5—

(1) After the definition of " component part " insert—

" conditional sale agreement " means an agreement for the
sale of goods under which the purchase price or part
of it is payable by instalments, and the property in the
goods is to remain in the seller (notwithstanding that
the buyer is to be in possession of the goods) until
such conditions as to the payment of instalments or
otherwise as may be specified in the agreement are
fulfilled ;

" hire agreement " means an agreement for the bailment or
(in Scotland) the hiring of goods which is not a hire-
purchase agreement ;

(2) for the definition of " credit-sale agreement " substitute—

" " credit sale agreement " means an agreement for the sale
of goods, under which the purchase price or part of it
is payable by instalments, but which is not a conditional
sale agreement ; "

(3) for the definition of " hire-purchase agreement "
substitute—

" " hire-purchase agreement " means an agreement, other
than a conditional sale agreement, under which—

(*a*) goods are bailed or (in Scotland) hired in
return for periodical payments by the person to
whom they are bailed or hired, and

(*b*) the property in the goods will pass to that
person if the terms of the agreement are complied
with and one or more of the following occurs—

(i) the exercise of an option to purchase by that
person,

          (ii) the doing of any other specified act by any party to the agreement,

          (iii) the happening of any other specified event ; "

Hire Purchase Act 1964

22. For Part III substitute the following (which reproduces the existing provisions of that Part subject only to changes in terminology)—

" PART III

TITLE TO MOTOR VEHICLES ON HIRE-PURCHASE OR CONDITIONAL SALE

Protection of purchasers of motor vehicles.
  27.—(1) This section applies where a motor vehicle has been bailed or (in Scotland) hired under a hire-purchase agreement, or has been agreed to be sold under a conditional sale agreement, and, before the property in the vehicle has become vested in the debtor, he disposes of the vehicle to another person.

(2) Where the disposition referred to in subsection (1) above is to a private purchaser, and he is a purchaser of the motor vehicle in good faith without notice of the hire-purchase or conditional sale agreement (the " relevant agreement ") that disposition shall have effect as if the creditor's title to the vehicle has been vested in the debtor immediately before that disposition.

(3) Where the person to whom the disposition referred to in subsection (1) above is made (the " original purchaser ") is a trade or finance purchaser, then if the person who is the first private purchaser of the motor vehicle after that disposition (the " first private purchaser ") is a purchaser of the vehicle in good faith without notice of the relevant agreement, the disposition of the vehicle to the first private purchaser shall have effect as if the title of the creditor to the vehicle had been vested in the debtor immediately before he disposed of it to the original purchaser.

(4) Where, in a case within subsection (3) above—

    (*a*) the disposition by which the first private purchaser becomes a purchaser of the motor vehicle in good faith without notice of the relevant agreement is itself a bailment or hiring under a hire-purchase agreement, and

    (*b*) the person who is the creditor in relation to that agreement disposes of the vehicle to the first private purchaser, or a person claiming under him, by transferring to him the property in the vehicle in pursuance of a provision in the agreement in that behalf,

the disposition referred to in paragraph (*b*) above (whether or not the person to whom it is made is a purchaser in good faith without notice of the relevant agreement) shall as well as the disposition referred to in paragraph (*a*) above, have effect as mentioned in sub-section (3) above.

(5) The preceding provisions of this section apply—

> (*a*) notwithstanding anything in section 21 of the Sale of Goods Act 1893 (sale of goods by a person not the owner), but

> (*b*) without prejudice to the provisions of the Factors Acts (as defined by section 62(1) of the said Act of 1893) or· of any other enactment enabling the apparent owner of goods to dispose of them as if he were the true owner.

(6) Nothing in this section shall exonerate the debtor from any liability (whether criminal or civil) to which he would be subject apart from this section ; and, in a case where the debtor disposes of the motor vehicle to a trade or finance purchaser, nothing in this section shall exonerate—

> (*a*) that trade or finance purchaser, or

> (*b*) any other trade or finance purchaser who becomes a purchaser of the vehicle and is not a person claiming under the first private purchaser,

from any liability (whether criminal or civil) to which he would be subject apart from this section.

Presumptions relating to dealings with motor vehicles.

28.—(1) Where in any proceedings (whether criminal or civil) relating to a motor vehicle it is proved—

> (*a*) that the vehicle was bailed or (in Scotland) hired under a hire-purchase agreement, or was agreed to be sold under a conditional sale agreement and

> (*b*) that a person (whether a party to the proceedings or not) became a private purchaser of the vehicle in good faith without notice of the hire-purchase or conditional sale agreement (the " relevant agreement "),

this section shall have effect for the purposes of the operation of section 27 of this Act in relation to those proceedings.

(2) It shall be presumed for those purposes, unless the contrary is proved, that the disposition of the vehicle to the person referred to in subsection (1)(*b*) above (the "relevant purchaser") was made by the debtor.

(3) If it is proved that that disposition was not made by the debtor, then it shall be presumed for those purposes, unless the contrary is proved—

> (*a*) that the debtor disposed of the vehicle to a private purchaser purchasing in good faith without notice of the relevant agreement, and

G

(b) that the relevant purchaser is or was a person claiming under the person to whom the debtor so disposed of the vehicle.

(4) If it is proved that the disposition of the vehicle to the relevant purchaser was not made by the debtor, and that the person to whom the debtor disposed of the vehicle (the " original purchaser ") was a trade or finance purchaser, then it shall be presumed for those purposes, unless the contrary is proved,

(a) that the person who, after the disposition of the vehicle to the original purchaser, first became a private purchaser of the vehicle was a purchaser in good faith without notice of the relevant agreement, and

(b) that the relevant purchaser is or was a person claiming under the original purchaser.

(5) Without prejudice to any other method of proof, where in any proceedings a party thereto admits a fact, that fact shall, for the purposes of this section, be taken as against him to be proved in relation to those proceedings.

Interpretation of Part III.

29.—(1) In this Part of this Act—

" conditional sale agreement " means an agreement for the sale of goods under which the purchase price or part of it is payable by instalments, and the property in the goods is to remain in the seller (notwithstanding that the buyer is to be in possession of the goods) until such conditions as to the payment of instalments or otherwise as may be specified in the agreement are fulfilled ;

" creditor " means the person by whom goods are bailed or (in Scotland) hired under a hire-purchase agreement or as the case may be, the seller under a conditional sale agreement, or the person to whom his rights and duties have passed by assignment or operation of law ;

" disposition " means any sale or contract of sale (including a conditional sale agreement), any bailment or (in Scotland) hiring under a hire-purchase agreement and any transfer of the property in goods in pursuance of a provision in that behalf contained in a hire-purchase agreement, and includes any transaction purporting to be a disposition (as so defined), and " dispose of " shall be construed accordingly ;

" hire-purchase agreement " means an agreement, other than a conditional sale agreement, under which—

(a) goods are bailed or (in Scotland) hired in return for periodical payments by the person to whom they are bailed or hired, and

(*b*) the property in the goods will pass to that person if the terms of the agreement are complied with and one or more of the following occurs—

(i) the exercise of an option to purchase by that person,

(ii) the doing of any other specified act by any party to the agreement,

(iii) the happening of any other specified events ; and

" motor vehicle " means a mechanically propelled vehicle intended or adapted for use on roads to which the public has access.

(2) In this Part of this Act " trade or finance purchaser " means a purchaser who, at the time of the disposition made to him, carries on a business which consists, wholly or partly,—

(*a*) of purchasing motor vehicles for the purpose of offering or exposing them for sale, or

(*b*) of providing finance by purchasing motor vehicles for the purpose of bailing or (in Scotland) hiring them under hire-purchase agreements or agreeing to sell them under conditional sale agreements,

and " private purchaser " means a purchaser who, at the time of the disposition made to him, does not carry on any such business.

(3) For the purposes of this Part of this Act a person becomes a purchaser of a motor vehicle if, and at the time when, a disposition of the vehicle is made to him ; and a person shall be taken to be a purchaser of a motor vehicle without notice of a hire-purchase agreement or conditional sale agreement if, at the time of the disposition made to him, he has no actual notice that the vehicle is or was the subject of any such agreement.

(4) In this Part of this Act the " debtor " in relation to a motor vehicle which has been bailed or hired under a hire-purchase agreement, or, as the case may be, agreed to be sold under a conditional sale agreement, means the person who at the material time (whether the agreement has before that time been terminated or not) either—

(*a*) is the person to whom the vehicle is bailed or hired under that agreement, or

(*b*) is, in relation to the agreement, the buyer,

including a person who at that time is, by virtue of section 130(4) of the Consumer Credit Act 1974 treated as a bailee or (in Scotland) a custodier of the vehicle.

(5) In this Part of this Act any reference to the title of the creditor to a motor vehicle which has been bailed or (in Scotland) hired under a hire-purchase agreement, or agreed to be sold under a conditional sale agreement, and is disposed of by the debtor, is a reference to such title (if any) to the vehicle as, immediately before that disposition, was vested in the person who then was the creditor in relation to the agreement,".

1964 c. 60.

Emergency Laws (Re-enactment and Repeals) Act 1964

23. In section 1—

(1) In subsection (1) for " or credit-sale agreements, or under agreements for letting on hire " substitute " conditional sale agreements, credit-sale agreements or hire agreements ".

(2) For subsection (2) substitute—

" (2) In this section—

" conditional sale agreement " means an agreement for the sale of any article under which the purchase price, or part of it is payable by instalments, and the property in the article is to remain in the seller (notwithstanding that the buyer is to be in possession of the article) until such conditions as to the payment of instalments or otherwise as may be specified in the agreement are fulfilled ;

" credit-sale agreement " means an agreement for the sale of any article, under which the purchase price or part of it is payable by instalments, but which is not a conditional sale agreement ;

" hire-purchase agreement " means an agreement, other than a conditional sale agreement under which—

(a) an article is bailed or (in Scotland) hired in return for periodical payments by the person to whom it is bailed or hired, and

(b) the property in the article will pass to that person if the terms of the agreement are complied with and one or more of the following occurs—

(i) the exercise of an option by that person ;

(ii) the doing of any other specified act by any party to the agreement ;

(iii) the happening of any other specified event ; and

" hire agreement " means an agreement for the bailment or (in Scotland) the hiring of an article which is not a hire-purchase agreement."

1964 c. 71.

Trading Stamps Act 1964

24. In section 2, for subsection (1) substitute—

" (1) No person shall after the coming into force of this section issue any trading stamp, or cause any trading stamp to be issued, or deliver any trading stamp to any person in connection with the sale of any goods, the bailment or (in Scotland) the hiring of any goods under a hire-purchase agreement or the performance of any services, unless such trading stamp bears on its face in clear and legible characters a value expressed in or by reference to current coin of the realm."

25. In section 3, for subsection (4) substitute—

" (4) In this section " redeemable trading stamps " means trading stamps delivered after the coming into force of this section in accordance with a trading stamp scheme on or in connection with either—

(*a*) the purchase of any goods,

(*b*) the bailment or (in Scotland) the hiring of any goods under a hire-purchase agreement, or

(*c*) the obtaining of any services for money,

and " the holder ", in relation to such a trading stamp, means the person to whom it was so delivered or any person who holds it without notice of any defect in title."

26. In section 10(1)—

(1) after the definition of " cash value " insert—

" " conditional sale agreement " means an agreement for the sale of goods under which the purchase price or part of it is payable by instalments, and the property in the goods is to remain in the seller (notwithstanding that the buyer is to be in possession of the goods) until such conditions as to the payment of instalments or otherwise as may be specified in the agreement are fulfilled ; ",
and

(2) after the definition of " goods " insert—

" " hire-purchase agreement " means an agreement, other than a conditional sale agrement, under which—

(*a*) goods are bailed or (in Scotland) hired in return for periodical payments by the person to whom they are bailed or hired, and

(*b*) the property in the goods will pass to that person if the terms of the agreement are complied with and one or more of the following occurs—

(i) the exercise of an option to purchase by that person,

(ii) the doing of any other specified act by any party to the agreement,

(iii) the happening of any other specified event ; ".

G 3

(3) For the definition of " trading stamp " substitute—

" " trading stamp " means a stamp which is, or is intended to be, delivered to any person on or in connection with either—

> (i) the purchase of any goods, or
>
> (ii) the bailment or (in Scotland) the hiring of any goods under a hire-purchase agreement,

(other than the purchase of a newspaper or other periodical of which the stamp forms part or in which it is contained) and is, or is intended to be, redeemable (whether singly or together with other such stamps) by that or some other person:

Provided that a stamp shall not be deemed to be a trading stamp if—

> (a) it is delivered or is intended to be delivered to a person (in this definition called " the purchaser ") on or in connection with the purchase of any goods by the purchaser, or the bailment or (in Scotland) the hiring to him of any goods, and
>
> (b) it is intended to be, and is not, redeemable from any person other than—
>
>> (i) the person (in this definition called " the seller ") from whom the purchaser purchased those goods, or who bailed or hired those goods to him, or
>>
>> (ii) any person from whom the seller (whether directly or indirectly) acquired those goods, and
>
> (c) in the case where a business is carried on by six or more retail establishments, the stamp is one of a kind obtainable at no more than six of those retail establishments, and not obtainable by the public elsewhere, and the arrangements under which it is redeemable are entirely separate from arrangements under which any other stamps, whether trading stamps or not, are redeemable,

and references in this definition to the purchase of goods include references to the obtaining of services for money ; ".

Housing (Scotland) Act 1966

27. In section 140(2), for the words from " as defined " onwards substitute " within the meaning of the Consumer Credit Act 1974 ".

Trade Descriptions Act 1968

28. In section 28, insert the following new subsection after subsection (5)—

" (5A) Subsection (5) of this section does not apply to disclosure for a purpose specified in section 174(3) of the Consumer Credit Act 1974."

Income and Corporation Taxes Act 1970

29. In section 495, for subsection (7) substitute—

" (7) In this section—

" hire-purchase agreement " means an agreement, other than a conditional sale agreement, under which—

(*a*) goods are bailed or (in Scotland) hired in return for periodical payments by the person to whom they are bailed or hired, and

(*b*) the property in the goods will pass to that person if the terms of the agreement are complied with and one or more of the following occurs—

(i) the exercise of an ᴓption to purchase by that person,

(ii) the doing of any other specified act by any party to the agreement,

(iii) the happening of any other specified event ; and

" conditional sale agreement " means an agreement for the sale of goods under which the purchase price or part of it is payable by instalments, and the property in the goods is to remain in the seller (notwithstanding that the buyer is to be in possession of the goods) until such conditions as to the payment of instalments or otherwise as may be specified in the agreement are fulfilled."

Administration of Justice Act 1970

30. After section 38 insert the following new section—

" 38A. This Part of this Act shall not apply to a mortgage securing an agreement which is a regulated agreement within the meaning of the Consumer Credit Act 1974."

31. In section 54(6)(*c*) after " 36 " insert " 38A ".

Vehicles (Excise) Act 1971

32. In section 38(1)—

(1) before the definition of " gas " insert—

" " conditional sale agreement " means an agreement for the sale of a vehicle under which the purchase price or part of it is payable by instalments, and the property in the vehicle is to remain in the seller (notwithstanding that the buyer is to be in possession of the vehicle) until such conditions as to the payment of instalments or otherwise as may be specified in the agreement are fulfilled ; "

(2) for the definition of " hackney carriage " substitute—

" hackney carriage " means a mechanically propelled vehicle standing or plying for hire and includes any mechanically propelled vehicle bailed or (in Scotland) hired under a hire agreement by a person whose trade it is to sell such vehicles or bail or hire them under hire agreements ;

(3) after the definition of " hackney carriage " insert—

" hire agreement " means an agreement for the bailment or (in Scotland) the hiring of a vehicle which is not a hire-purchase agreement ;

" hire-purchase agreement " means an agreement, other than a conditional sale agreement, under which—

(*a*) a vehicle is bailed or (in Scotland) hired in return for periodical payments by the person to whom it is bailed or hired, and

(*b*) the property in the vehicle will pass to that person if the terms of the agreement are complied with and one or more of the following occurs—

(i) the exercise of an option to purchase by that person,

(ii) the doing of any other specified act by any party to the agreement,

(iii) the happening of any other specified event ; ".

Industry Act 1972

33. In section 6(2)—

(1) After the definition of " " capital expenditure ", or expenditure of a " capital nature " " " insert—

" conditional sale agreement " means an agreement for the sale of goods under which the purchase price or part of it is payable by instalments, and the property in the goods is to remain in the seller (notwithstanding that the buyer is to be in possession of the goods) until such conditions as to the payment of instalments or otherwise as may be specified in the agreement are fulfilled ; " and

(2) For the definition of " hire-purchase agreement " substitute—

" " hire-purchase agreement " means an agreement, other than a conditional sale agreement, under which

(*a*) goods are bailed or (in Scotland) hired in return for periodical payments by the person to whom they are bailed or hired, and

(*b*) the property in the goods will pass to that person if the terms of the agreement are complied with and one or more of the following occurs—

(i) the exercise of an option to purchase by that person,

(ii) the doing of any other specified act by any party to the agreement,

(iii) the happening of any other specified event ; ".

Counter-Inflation Act 1973

34. In section 21(5)—

(*a*) for " total purchase price or hire-purchase price " substitute
" total price " ; and

(*b*) for the words from " This subsection " onwards substitute—
" In this subsection—

" conditional sale agreement " means an agreement
for the sale of goods under which the purchase
price or part of it is payable by instalments,
and the property in the goods is to remain in
the seller (notwithstanding that the buyer is
to be in possession of the goods) until such
conditions as to the payment of instalments
or otherwise as may be specified in the agreement are fulfilled, and

" hire-purchase agreement " means an agreement,
other than a conditional sale agreement, under
which—

(*a*) goods are bailed or (in Scotland) hired
in return for periodical payments by the
person to whom they are bailed or hired, and

(*b*) the property in the goods will pass to
that person if the terms of the agreement are
complied with and one or more of the
following occurs—

(i) the exercise of an option to purchase
by that person,

(ii) the doing of any other specified act
by any party to the agreement,

(iii) the happening of any other specified
event ; and

" total price " means the total sum payable by the
person to whom goods are bailed or hired under
a hire-purchase agreement or, as the case may
be, the buyer under a conditional sale agreement including any sum payable on the exercise
of an option to purchase but excluding any
sum payable as a penalty or as compensation or
damages for a breach of the agreement."

Supply of Goods (Implied Terms) Act 1973

35. For sections 8 to 12 substitute the following sections (which
reproduce the existing provisions of those sections subject only to
changes in terminology)—

"Implied
terms as
to title.

8.—(1) In every hire-purchase agreement, other than
one to which subsection (2) below applies, there is—

(*a*) an implied condition on the part of the creditor
that he will have a right to sell the goods at the
time when the property is to pass ; and

(*b*) an implied warranty that—

(i) the goods are free, and will remain free until the time when the property is to pass, from any charge or encumbrance not disclosed or known to the person to whom the goods are bailed or (in Scotland) hired before the agreement is made, and

(ii) that person will enjoy quiet possession of the goods except so far as it may be disturbed by any person entitled to the benefit of any charge or encumbrance so disclosed or known.

(2) In a hire-purchase agreement, in the case of which there appears from the agreement or is to be inferred from the circumstances of the agreement an intention that the creditor should transfer only such title as he or a third person may have, there is—

(*a*) an implied warranty that all charges or encumbrances known to the creditor and not known to the person to whom the goods are bailed or hired have been disclosed to that person before the agreement is made ; and

(*b*) an implied warranty that neither—

(i) the creditor ; nor

(ii) in a case where the parties to the agreement intend that any title which may be transferred shall be only such title as a third person may have, that person ; nor

(iii) anyone claiming through or under the creditor or that third person otherwise than under a charge or encumbrance disclosed or known to the person to whom the goods are bailed or hired, before the agreement is made ;

will disturb the quiet possession of the person to whom the goods are bailed or hired.

Bailing or hiring by description.

9.—(1) Where under a hire-purchase agreement goods are bailed or (in Scotland) hired by description, there is an implied condition that the goods will correspond with the description, and if under the agreement the goods are bailed or hired by reference to a sample as well as a description, it is not sufficient that the bulk of the goods corresponds with the sample if the goods do not also correspond with the description.

(2) Goods shall not be prevented from being bailed or hired by description by reason only that, being exposed for sale, bailment or hire, they are selected by the person to whom they are bailed or hired.

Implied
undertakings
as to quality
or fitness.

10.—(1) Except as provided by this section and section 11 below and subject to the provisions of any other enactment, including any enactment of the Parliament of Northern Ireland or the Northern Ireland Assembly, there is no implied condition or warranty as to the quality or fitness for any particular purpose of goods bailed or (in Scotland) hired under a hire-purchase agreement.

(2) Where the creditor bails or hires goods under a hire-purchase agreement in the course of a business, there is an implied condition that the goods are of merchantable quality, except that there is no such condition—

    (*a*) as regards defects specifically drawn to the attention of the person to whom the goods are bailed or hired before the agreement is made ; or

    (*b*) if that person examines the goods before the agreement is made, as regards defects which that examination ought to reveal.

(3) Where the creditor bails or hires goods under a hire-purchase agreement in the course of a business and the person to whom the goods are bailed or hired, expressly or by implication, makes known—

    (*a*) to the creditor in the course of negotiations conducted by the creditor in relation to the making of the hire-purchase agreement, or

    (*b*) to a credit-broker in the course of negotiations conducted by that broker in relation to goods sold by him to the creditor before forming the subject matter of the hire-purchase agreement,

any particular purpose for which the goods are being bailed or hired, there is an implied condition that the goods supplied under the agreement are reasonably fit for that purpose, whether or not that is a purpose for which such goods are commonly supplied, except where the circumstances show that the person to whom the goods are bailed or hired does not rely, or that it is unreasonable for him to rely, on the skill or judgment of the creditor or credit-broker.

(4) An implied condition or warranty as to quality or fitness for a particular purpose may be annexed to a hire-purchase agreement by usage.

(5) The preceding provisions of this section apply to a hire-purchase agreement made by a person who in the course of a business is acting as agent for the creditor as they apply to an agreement made by the creditor in the course of a business, except where the creditor is not bailing or hiring in the course of a business and either the person to whom the goods are bailed or hired knows that fact or reasonable steps are taken to bring it to the notice of that person before the agreement is made.

SCH. 4

(6) In subsection (3) above and this subsection—

    (*a*) " credit-broker " means a person acting in the course of a business of credit brokerage ;

    (*b*) " credit brokerage " means the effecting of introductions of individuals desiring to obtain credit—

        (i) to persons carrying on any business so far as it relates to the provision of credit, or

        (ii) to other persons engaged in credit brokerage.

Samples.

11. Where under a hire-purchase agreement goods are bailed or (in Scotland) hired by reference to a sample, there is an implied condition—

    (*a*) that the bulk will correspond with the sample in quality ; and

    (*b*) that the person to whom the goods are bailed or hired will have a reasonable opportunity of comparing the bulk with the sample ; and

    (*c*) that the goods will be free from any defect, rendering them unmerchantable, which would not be apparent on reasonable examination of the sample.

Exclusion of implied terms and conditions.

12.—(1) An express condition or warranty does not negative a condition or warranty implied by this Act unless inconsistent with it.

(2) A term of a hire-purchase agreement or any other agreement exempting from all or any of the provisions of section 8 above shall be void.

(3) A term of a hire-purchase agreement or any other agreement exempting from all or any of the provisions of sections 9, 10 or 11 above shall be void in the case of a consumer agreement and shall, in any other case, not be enforceable to the extent that it is shown that it would not be fair or reasonable to allow reliance on the term.

(4) In determining for the purpose of subsection (3) above whether or not reliance on any such term would be fair or reasonable regard shall be had to all the circumstances of the case and in particular to the following matters—

    (*a*) the strength of the bargaining positions of the creditor and the person to whom the goods are bailed or hired relative to each other, taking into account, among other things, the availability of suitable alternative products and sources of supply ;

    (*b*) whether that person received an inducement to agree to the term or in accepting it had an opportunity of acquiring the goods or suitable alternatives without it from any source of supply ;

(*c*) whether that person knew or ought reasonably to have known of the existence and extent of the term (having regard, among other things, to any custom of the trade and any previous course of dealing between the parties) ;

(*d*) where the term exempts from all or any of the provisions of sections 9, 10 or 11 above if some condition is not complied with, whether it was reasonable at the time of the agreement to expect that compliance with that condition would be practicable ;

(*e*) whether the goods were manufactured, processed or adapted to the special order of that person.

(5) Subsection (4) above shall not prevent the court from holding, in accordance with any rule of law, that a term which purports to exclude or restrict any of the provisions of sections 9, 10 and 11 above is not a term of the hire-purchase agreement.

(6) In this section " consumer agreement " means a hire-purchase agreement where the creditor makes the agreement in the course of a business and the goods to which the agreement relates—

(*a*) are of a type ordinarily supplied for private use or consumption ; and

(*b*) are bailed or (in Scotland) hired to a person who does not bail or hire them or hold himself out as bailing or hiring them in the course of a business.

(7) The onus of proving that a hire-purchase agreement is to be treated for the purposes of this section as not being a consumer agreement shall lie on the party so contending.

(8) Any reference in this section to a term exempting from all or any of the provisions of any section of this Act is a reference to a term which purports to exclude or restrict, or has the effect of excluding or restricting, the operation of all or any of the provisions of that section, or the exercise of a right conferred by any provision of that section, or any liability of the owner for breach of a condition or warranty implied by any provision of that section.

(9) It is hereby declared that any reference in this section to a term of an agreement includes a reference to a term which although not contained in an agreement is incorporated in the agreement by another term of the agreement."

36. For sections 14 and 15 substitute the following sections (which reproduce the existing provisions of those sections subject only to changes in terminology)—

"Special provisions as to conditional sale agreements.   14.—(1) Section 11(1)(c) of the principal Act (whereby in certain circumstances a breach of a condition in a contract of sale is treated only as a breach of warranty) shall not apply to conditional sale agreements which are agreements for consumer sales.

(2) In England and Wales and Northern Ireland a breach of a condition (whether express or implied) to be fulfilled by the seller under any such agreement shall be treated as a breach of warranty, and not as grounds for rejecting the goods and treating the agreement as repudiated, if (but only if) it would have fallen to be so treated had the condition been contained or implied in a corresponding hire-purchase agreement as a condition to be fulfilled by the creditor.

Supplementary.   15.—(1) In sections 8 to 14 above and this section—

" business " includes a profession and the activities of any government department (including a Northern Ireland department), local authority or statutory undertaker ;

" buyer " and " seller " includes a person to whom rights and duties under a conditional sale agreement have passed by assignment or operation of law ;

" condition " and " warranty ", in relation to Scotland, mean stipulation, and any stipulation referred to in sections 8(1)(a), 9, 10 and 11 above shall be deemed to be material to the agreement.

" conditional sale agreement " means an agreement for the sale of goods under which the purchase price or part of it is payable by instalments, and the property in the goods is to remain in the seller (notwithstanding that the buyer is to be in possession of the goods) until such conditions as to the payment of instalments or otherwise as may be specified in the agreement are fulfilled ;

" consumer sale " has the same meaning as in section 55 of the principal Act, as amended by section 4 above ;

" creditor " means the person by whom the goods are bailed or (in Scotland) hired under a hire-purchase agreement or the person to whom his rights and duties under the agreement have passed by assignment or operation of law ; and "hire-purchase agreement" means an agreement, other than conditional sale agreement, under which—

>   (*a*) goods are bailed or (in Scotland) hired in return for periodical payments by the person to whom they are bailed or hired, and
>
>   (*b*) the property in the goods will pass to that person if the terms of the agreement are complied with and one or more of the following occurs—
>
>>   (i) the exercise of an option to purchase by that person,
>>
>>   (ii) the doing of any other specified act by any party to the agreement,
>>
>>   (iii) the happening of any other specified event.

(2) Goods of any kind are of merchantable quality within the meaning of section 10(2) above if they are as fit for the purpose or purposes for which goods of that kind are commonly bought as it is reasonable to expect having regard to any description applied to them, the price (if relevant) and all the other relevant circumstances ; and in section 11 above "unmerchantable" shall be construed accordingly.

(3) In section 14(2) above "corresponding hire-purchase agreement" means, in relation to a conditional sale agreement, a hire-purchase agreement relating to the same goods as the conditional sale agreement and made between the same parties and at the same time and in the same circumstances and, as nearly as may be, in the same terms as the conditional sale agreement.

(4) Nothing in sections 8 to 13 above shall prejudice the operation of any other enactment including any enactment of the Parliament of Northern Ireland or the Northern Ireland Assembly or any rule of law whereby any condition or warranty, other than one relating to quality or fitness, is to be implied in any hire-purchase agreement."

Fair Trading Act 1973

1973 c. 41.

37. For section 138(5) substitute—

"(5) In subsection (4) of this section, the following expressions have the meanings given by, or referred to in, section 189 of the Consumer Credit Act 1974—

> "antecedent negotiations",
>
> "conditional sale agreement",
>
> "credit-sale agreement",
>
> "hire-purchase agreement"."

PART II

                       NORTHERN IRELAND

Irish Bankrupt and Insolvent Act 1857

38. The following section shall be inserted after section 313—

"Hire-
purchase
etc.
agreements.

313A.—(1) Goods—

(*a*) bailed under a hire-purchase agreement or a consumer hire agreement, or

(*b*) agreed to be sold under a conditional sale agreement, or

(*c*) subject to a regulated agreement under which a bill of sale is given by way of security,

shall not during the period between—

(i) the service of a default notice under the Consumer Credit Act 1974 in respect of the goods, and

(ii) the date on which the notice expires or is earlier complied with,

be treated for the purposes of section 313 of this Act as goods which are by the consent and permission of the creditor, or (in the case of goods which are the subject of a consumer hir agreement) of the owner, in the possession, order or disposition of the person to whom they are bailed or agreed to be sold or who is the grantor of the bill of sale.

(2) In this section—

" conditional sale agreement " means an agreement for the sale of goods under which the purchase price or part of it is payable by instalments, and the property in the goods is to remain in the seller (notwithstanding that the buyer is to be in possession of the goods) until such conditions as to the payment of instalments or otherwise as may be specified in the agreement are fulfilled ;

" consumer hire agreement " has the meaning given by section 15 of the Consumer Credit Act 1974 ;

" creditor " means the person bailing goods under a hire-purchase agreement or, as the case may be, the seller under a conditional sale agreement or the person providing credit under a regulated agreement, and includes the person to whom his rights and duties under the agreement have passed by assignment or operation of law ;

" owner " means a person who bails out goods under a consumer hire agreement or the person to whom his rights and duties under the agreement have been passed by assignment or operation of law ; and

" regulated agreement " has the meaning given by section 189 of the Consumer Credit Act 1974." ;

" hire-purchase agreement " means an agreement, other than a conditional sale agreement, under which—

(*a*) goods are bailed or (in Scotland) hired in return for periodical payments by the person to whom they are bailed or hired, and

(*b*) the property in the goods will pass to that person if the terms of the agreement are complied with and one or more of the following occurs—

(i) the exercise of an option to purchase by that person,

(ii) the doing of any other specified act by any party to the agreement,

(iii) the happening of any other specified event."

Bills of Sale (Ireland) Act (1879) Amendment Act 1883   1883 c. 7.

39. The following section shall be inserted after section 7 : —

"Defaults under consumer credit agreements.   7A.—(1) Paragraph (1) of section 7 of this Act does not apply to a default relating to a bill of sale given by way of security for the payment of money under a regulated agreement to which section 87(1) of the Consumer Credit Act 1974 applies : —

(*a*) unless the restriction imposed by section 88(2) of that Act has ceased to apply to the bill of sale ; or

(*b*) if, by virtue of section 89 of that Act, the default is to be treated as not having occurred.

(2) Where paragraph (1) of section 7 of this Act does apply in relation to a bill of sale such as is mentioned in subsection (1) of this section, the proviso to that section shall have effect with the insertion after " High Court " of the words " or county court ".

Liability for War Damage (Miscellaneous Provisions) Act (Northern Ireland) 1939   1939 c. 36 (N.I.).

40. In section 1(3), for paragraph (*a*) and (*b*) substitute—

" (*a*) a hire-purchase agreement or a conditional sale agreement within the meaning of the Consumer Credit Act 1974 being a consumer credit agreement as defined by that Act ; or

(*b*) a consumer hire agreement within the meaning of that Act."

Clean Air Act (Northern Ireland) 1964

41. In section 14(4) for " a hire-purchase agreement for the letting to him " substitute—" either—

    (i) a conditional sale agreement for the sale to him, or

    (ii) a hire-purchase agreement for the bailment to him,".

42. In section 43(1)—

    (*a*) after the definition of " chimney " insert—

      " " conditional sale agreement " means an agreement for the sale of goods under which the purchase price or part of it is payable by instalments, and the property in the goods is to remain in the seller (notwithstanding that the buyer is to be in possession of the goods) until such conditions as to the payment of instalments or otherwise as may be specified in the agreement are fulfilled ; ", and

    (*b*) for the definition of " hire-purchase agreement " substitute—

      " " hire purchase agreement " means an agreement, other than a conditional sale agreement, under which—

        (*a*) goods are bailed in return for periodical payments by the person to whom they are bailed, and

        (*b*) the property in the goods will pass to that person if the terms of the agreement are complied with and one or more of the following occurs—

          (i) the exercise of an option to purchase by that person,

          (ii) the doing of any other specified act by any party to the agreement,

          (iii) the happening of any other specified event ; ".

Trading Stamps Act (Northern Ireland) 1965

43. In section 2, for subsection (1) substitute—

    " (1) No person shall after the coming into force of this section issue any trading stamp, or cause any trading stamp to be issued, or deliver any trading stamp to any person in connection with the sale of any goods, the bailment of any goods under a hire-purchase agreement or the performance of any services, unless such trading stamp bears on its face in clear and legible characters a value expressed in or by reference to current coin of the realm ".

44. In section 3, for subsection (4) substitute—

    " (4) In this section " redeemable trading stamps " means trading stamps delivered after the coming into force of this section in accordance with a trading stamp scheme on or in connection with either—

    (*a*) the purchase of any goods,

    (*b*) the bailment of any goods under a hire-purchase agreement, or

(c) the obtaining of any services for money,
and " the holder " in relation to such a trading stamp, means
the person to whom it was so delivered or any person who holds
it without notice of any defect in title."

45. In section 9—

(1) after the definition of " cash value " insert—

" " conditional sale agreement " means an agreement for the
sale of goods under which the purchase price or part
of it is payable by instalments, and the property in
the goods is to remain in the seller (notwithstanding
that the buyer is to be in possession of the goods) until
such conditions as to the payment of instalments or
otherwise as may be specified in the agreement are
fulfilled ; ", and

(2) after the definition of " goods " insert—

" " hire-purchase agreement " means an agreement, other
than a conditional sale agreement, under which—

(a) goods are bailed in return for periodical payments by the person to whom they are bailed, and

(b) the property in the goods will pass to that
person if the terms of the agreement are complied
with and one or more of the following occurs—

(i) the exercise of an option to purchase by that
person,

(ii) the doing of any other specified act by any
party to the agreement,

(iii) the happening of any other specified event : "

(3) For the definition of " trading stamp " substitute—

" " trading stamp " means a stamp which is, or is intended
to be, delivered to any person on or in connection with
either—

(i) the purchase of any goods, or

(ii) the bailment of any goods under a hire-
purchase agreement,

(other than the purchase of a newspaper or other
periodical of which the stamp forms part or in which
it is contained) and is, or is intended to be, redeemable
(whether singly or together with other such stamps) by
that or some other person:

Provided that a stamp shall not be deemed to be a trading
stamp if—

(a) it is delivered or is intended to be delivered to
a person (in this definition called " the purchaser ")
on or in connection with the purchase of any goods
by the purchaser, or the bailment to him of any
goods, and

      (*b*) it is intended to be, and is not, redeemable from any person other than—

          (i) the person (in this definition called " the seller ") from whom the purchaser purchased those goods or who bailed those goods to him, or

          (ii) any person from whom the seller (whether directly or indirectly) acquired those goods, and

      (*c*) in the case where a business is carried on by six or more retail establishments, the stamp is one of a kind obtainable at no more than six of those retail establishments, and not obtainable by the public elsewhere, and the arrangements under which it is redeemable are entirely separate from arrangements under which any other stamps, whether trading stamps or not, are redeemable,

and references in this definition to the purchase of goods include references to the obtaining of services for money.".

Consumer Protection Act (Northern Ireland) 1965

46. In section 2, for subsections (5) and (6) substitute—

" (5) If as respects goods of any class or description regulations under section 1 so provide, subsections (1) to (3) (other than subsection 3(*d*) and (*e*)) shall apply subject to subsection (6) in relation to goods of that class or description as if—

      (*a*) references to selling or to a sale included references to—

          (i) bailing under a hire-purchase agreement, or

          (ii) bailing under a hire agreement, or

          (iii) an agreement to sell under a conditional sale agreement ; and

      (*b*) the reference to a sale under a credit-sale agreement were a reference—

          (i) to a bailment under a hire-purchase agreement, or

          (ii) to an agreement to sell under a conditional sale agreement.

(6) Subsections (1) and (2) shall not apply—

      (*a*) in a case of bailment under a hire agreement, where the bailment is incidental to an agreement under which payments are to be made in the form of rent issuing out of land ;

      (*b*) in a case of possession for the purpose of bailment under a hire agreement, where possession is for the purpose of a bailment which is incidental to an agreement under which payments are to be made in the form of rent issuing out of land ;

      (*c*) in any case of bailment under a hire agreement, where the bailment was lawful at the time when it began."

SCH. 4

47. In section 5—

(1) after the definition of " component part " insert—

" " conditional sale agreement " means an agreement for the sale of goods under which the purchase price or part of it is payable by instalments, and the property in the goods is to remain in the seller (notwithstanding that the buyer is to be in possession of the goods) until such conditions as to the payment of instalments or otherwise as may be specified in the agreement are fulfilled ;

" hire agreement " means an agreement for the bailment of goods which is not a hire-purchase agreement ; "

(2) for the definition of " credit-sale agreement " substitute—

" " credit sale agreement " means an agreement for the sale of goods, under which the purchase price or part of it is payable by instalments, but which is not a conditional sale agreement ; "

(3) for the definition of hire-purchase agreement substitute—

" " hire-purchase agreement " means an agreement, other than a conditional sale agreement, under which—

(*a*) goods are bailed in return for periodical payments by the person to whom they are bailed, and

(*b*) the property in the goods will pass to that person if the terms of the agreement are complied with and one or more of the following occurs—

(i) the exercise of an option to purchase by that person,

(ii) the doing of any other specified act by any party to the agreement,

(iii) the happening of any other specified event ; ".

Industrial Investment (General Assistance) Act (Northern Ireland) 1966   1966 c. 41 (N.I.).

48. In section 14(1)—

(1) after the definition of " computer " insert—

" " conditional sale agreement " means an agreement for the sale of goods under which the purchase price or part of it is payable by instalments, and the property in the goods is to remain in the seller (notwithstanding that the buyer is to be in possession of the goods) until such conditions as to the payment of instalments or otherwise as may be specified in the agreement are fulfilled ; " and

(2) for the definition of " hire-purchase agreement " substitute—

" " hire-purchase agreement " means an agreement, other than a conditional sale agreement, under which—

(*a*) goods are bailed in return for periodical payments by the person to whom they are bailed or hired, and

　　(*b*) the property in the goods will pass to that person if the terms of the agreement are complied with and one or more of the following occurs—

　　　(i) the exercise of an option to purchase by that person,

　　　(ii) the doing of any other specified act by any party to the agreement,

　　　(iii) the happening of any other specified event ; ".

1966 c. 42 (N.I.).

Hire-Purchase Act (*Northern Ireland*) 1966

49. For Part VI substitute the following (which reproduces the existing provisions of that Part subject only to changes in terminology)—

" PART VI

TITLE TO MOTOR VEHICLES ON HIRE-PURCHASE OR CONDITIONAL SALE

Protection of purchasers of motor vehicles.

62.—(1) This section applies where a motor vehicle has been bailed under a hire-purchase agreement, or has been agreed to be sold under a conditional sale agreement, and, before the property in the vehicle has become vested in the debtor, he disposes of the vehicle to another person.

(2) Where the disposition referred to in subsection (1) is to a private purchaser, and he is a purchaser of the motor vehicle in good faith without notice of the hire-purchase or conditional sale agreement (the " relevant agreement ") that disposition shall have effect as if the creditor's title to the vehicle had been vested in the debtor immediately before that disposition.

(3) Where the person to whom the disposition referred to in subsection (1) is made (the " original purchaser ") is a trade or finance purchaser, then if the person who is the first private purchaser of the motor vehicle after that disposition (" the first private purchaser ") is a purchaser of the vehicle in good faith without notice of the relevant agreement, the disposition of the vehicle to the first private purchaser shall have effect as if the title of the creditor to the vehicle had been vested in the debtor immediately before he disposed of it to the original purchaser.

(4) Where, in a case within subsection (3)—

　　(*a*) the disposition by which the first private purchaser becomes a purchaser of the motor vehicle in good faith without notice of the relevant agreement is itself a bailment under a hire-purchase agreement, and

　　(*b*) the person who is the creditor in relation to that agreement disposes of the vehicle to the first private purchaser, or a person claiming under him, by transferring to him the property in the vehicle in pursuance of a provision in the agreement in that behalf,

the disposition referred to in paragraph (*b*) (whether or not the person to whom it is made is a purchaser in good faith without notice of the relevant agreement) shall, as well as the disposition referred to in paragraph (*a*), have effect as mentioned in subsection (3).

(5) The preceding provisions of this section apply—

(*a*) notwithstanding anything in section 21 of the Sale of Goods Act 1893 (sale of goods by a person not the owner), but

(*b*) without prejudice to the provisions of the Factors Act (as defined by section 62(1) of the said Act of 1893) or of any other enactment enabling the apparent owner of goods to dispose of them as if he were the true owner.

(6) Nothing in this section shall exonerate the debtor from any liability (whether criminal or civil) to which he would be subject apart from this section; and, in a case where the debtor disposes of the motor vehicle to a trade or finance purchaser, nothing in this section shall exonerate—

(*a*) that trade or finance purchaser, or

(*b*) any other trade or finance purchaser who becomes a purchaser of the vehicle and is not a person claiming under the first private purchaser,

from any liability (whether criminal or civil) to which he would be subject apart from this section.

Presumptions relating to dealings with motor vehicles.

63.—(1) Where in any proceedings (whether criminal or civil) relating to a motor vehicle it is proved—

(*a*) that the vehicle was bailed under a hire-purchase agreement, or was agreed to be sold under a conditional sale agreement, and

(*b*) that a person (whether a party to the proceedings or not) became a private purchaser of the vehicle in good faith without notice of the hire-purchase or conditional sale agreement (the " relevant agreement "),

this section shall have effect for the purpose of the operation of section 62 of this Act in relation to those proceedings.

(2) It shall be presumed for those purposes, unless the contrary is proved, that the disposition of the vehicle to the person referred to in subsection (1)(*b*) (the " relevant purchaser ") was made by the debtor.

(3) If it is proved that that disposition was not made by the debtor, then it shall be presumed for those purposes, unless the contrary is proved—

 (a) that the debtor disposed of the vehicle to a private purchaser purchasing in good faith without notice of the relevant agreement, and

 (b) that the relevant purchaser is or was a person claiming under the person to whom the debtor so disposed of the vehicle.

(4) If it is proved that the disposition of the vehicle to the relevant purchaser was not made by the debtor, and that the person to whom the debtor disposed of the vehicle (the "original purchaser") was a trade or finance purchaser, then it shall be presumed for those purposes, unless the contrary is proved,—

 (a) that the person who, after the disposition of the vehicle to the original purchaser, first became a private purchaser of the vehicle was a purchaser in good faith without notice of the relevant agreement, and

 (b) that the relevant purchaser is or was a person claiming under the original purchaser.

(5) Without prejudice to any other method of proof, where in any proceedings a party thereto admits a fact, that fact shall, for the purposes of this section, be taken as against him to be proved in relation to those proceedings.

Interpretation of Part VI and application to the Crown.

64.—(1) In this Part—

"conditional sale agreement" means an agreement for the sale of goods under which the purchase price or part of it is payable by instalments, and the property in the goods is to remain in the seller (notwithstanding that the buyer is to be in possession of the goods) until such conditions as to the payment of instalments or otherwise as may be specified in the agreement are fulfilled ;

"creditor" means the person by whom goods are bailed under a hire-purchase agreement or, as the case may be, the seller under a conditional sale agreement, or the person to whom his rights and duties have passed by assignment or operation of law ;

"disposition" means any sale or contract of sale (including a conditional sale agreement), any bailment under a hire-purchase agreement and any transfer of the property in goods in pursuance of a provision in that behalf contained in a hire-purchase agreement, and includes any transaction purporting to be a disposition (as so defined), and "dispose of" shall be construed accordingly ;

" hire-purchase agreement " means an agreement,   Sch. 4
other than a conditional sale agreement, under
which—

     (*a*) goods are bailed in return for periodical
payments by the person to whom they are
bailed, and

     (*b*) the property in the goods will pass to
that person if the terms of the agreement
are complied with and one or more of the
following occurs—

         (i) the exercise of an option to purchase
by that person,

         (ii) the doing of any other specified act
by any party to the agreement,

         (iii) the happening of any other specified
event ; and

" motor vehicle " means a mechanically propelled
vehicle intended or adapted for use on roads
to which the public has access.

(2) In this Part " trade or finance purchaser " means
a purchaser who, at the time of the disposition made
to him, carries on a business which consists, wholly or
partly,—

     (*a*) of purchasing motor vehicles for the purpose of
offering or exposing them for sale, or

     (*b*) of providing finance by purchasing motor vehicles
for the purpose of bailing them under hire-
purchase agreements or agreeing to sell them
under conditional sale agreements,

and " private purchaser " means a purchaser who, at
the time of the disposition made to him, does not carry
on any such business.

(3) For the purposes of this Part a person becomes
a purchaser of a motor vehicle if, and at the time when,
a disposition of the vehicle is made to him ; and a
person shall be taken to be a purchaser of a motor
vehicle without notice of a hire-purchase agreement or
conditional sale agreement if, at the time of the disposition made to him, he has no actual notice that the
vehicle is or was the subject of any such agreement.

(4) In this Part the " debtor ", in relation to a motor
vehicle which has been bailed under a hire-purchase
agreement or, as the case may be, agreed to be sold
under a conditional sale agreement, means the person who
at the material time (whether the agreement has before
that time been terminated or not) either—

     (*a*) is the person to whom the vehicle is bailed
under that agreement or

     (*b*) is, in relation to the agreement, the buyer,
including a person who at that time is, by virtue
of section 130(4) of the Consumer Credit Act
1974 treated as a bailee of the vehicle.

(5) In this Part any reference to the title of the creditor to a motor vehicle which has been bailed under a hire-purchase agreement, or agreed to be sold under a conditional sale agreement, and is disposed of by the debtor, is a reference to such title (if any) to the vehicle as, immediately before that disposition, was vested in the person who then was the creditor in relation to the agreement.

(6) This Part binds the Crown to the full extent authorised or permitted by the constitutional laws of Northern Ireland.".

Vehicles (Excise) Act (Northern Ireland) 1972

50. In section 35(1)—

(*a*) before the definition of " gas " insert—

" " conditional sale agreement " means an agreement for the sale of a vehicle under which the purchase price or part of it is payable by instalments, and the property in the vehicle is to remain in the seller (notwithstanding that the buyer is to be in possession of the vehicle) until such conditions as to the payment of instalments or otherwise as may be specified in the agreement are fulfilled ; ".

(*b*) for the definition of " hackney carriage " substitute—

" " hackney carriage " means a mechanically propelled vehicle standing or plying for hire and includes any mechanically propelled vehicle bailed under a hire agreement by a person whose trade it is to sell such vehicles or bail them under hire agreements ; ".

(*c*) After the definition of " hackney carriage " insert—

" " hire agreement " means an agreement for the bailment of a vehicle which is not a hire-purchase agreement ;

" hire-purchase agreement " means an agreement, other than a conditional sale agreement, under which—

(*a*) a vehicle is bailed in return for periodical payments by the person to whom it is bailed, and

(*b*) the property in the vehicle will pass to that person if the terms of the agreement are complied with and one or more of the following occurs—

(i) the exercise of an option to purchase by that person,

(ii) the doing of any other specified act by any party to the agreement,

(iii) the happening of any other specified event ;".

Miscellaneous Transferred Excise Duties Act (Northern Ireland) 1972

51. In section 1(2) for " VII " where first occurring substitute " V " and for " to VII " where secondly occurring substitute " and V ".

SCHEDULE 5
REPEALS
PART I
UNITED KINGDOM

Section 192 (3)(*b*).

Chapter	Short Title	Extent of Repeal
1835 (5 & 6 Will. 4.) c. 62.	Statutory Declarations Act 1835.	Section 12.
1839 (2 & 3 Vict.) c. 47.	Metropolitan Police Act 1839.	Section 50.
1839 (2 & 3 Vict.) c. 71.	Police Courts (Metropolis) Act 1839.	In section 27 the words " pawned, pledged " and the words " or of any person who shall have advanced money upon the credit of such goods ". In section 28 the words " pawned, pledged or " (in each place).
1872 (35 & 36 Vict.) c. 93.	Pawnbrokers Act 1872.	The whole Act.
1875 (38 & 39 Vict.) c. 25.	Public Stores Act 1875.	In section 9 the words " or a pawnbroker " and " or to pawnbrokers ".
1891 (54 & 55 Vict.) c. 50.	Commissioners for Oaths Act 1891.	In section 1, the words " or the Pawnbrokers Act 1872 ".
1892 (55 & 56 Vict.) c. 4.	Betting and Loans (Infants) Act 1892.	Sections 2 to 4. Section 6, except as far as it extends to Northern Ireland. In section 7, the definitions of " indictment " and " summary conviction ".
1892 (55 & 56 Vict.) c. 55.	Burgh Police (Scotland) Act 1892.	In section 453, the words " and all offences committed against the provisions of the Pawnbrokers Act 1872,".
1894 (56 & 57 Vict.) c. 71.	Sale of Goods Act 1893.	Section 14(6).
1894 (56 & 57 Vict.) c. 73.	Local Government Act 1894.	Section 27(1)(*b*).
1897 (60 & 61 Vict.) c. 30.	Police (Property) Act 1897.	In section 1(1), the words " or section thirty-four of the Pawnbrokers Act 1872 ".
1900 (63 & 64 Vict.) c. 51.	Moneylenders Act 1900.	The whole Act.
1908 (8 Edw. 7.) c. 53.	Law of Distress Amendment Act 1908.	In section 4(1) the words " bill of sale, hire purchase agreement or ".
1927 (17 & 18 Geo. 5.) c. 21.	Moneylenders Act 1927.	The whole Act.
1933 (23 & 24 Geo. 5.) c. 12.	Children and Young Persons Act 1933.	Section 8.

Chapter	Short Title	Extent of Repeal
1937 (1 Edw. 8 & 1 Geo. 6.) c. 37.	Children and Young Persons (Scotland) Act 1937.	Section 19.
1939 (2 & 3 Geo. 6.) c. 75.	Compensation (Defence) Act 1939.	In section 18(1) the words from " the expression ' hire purchase agreement ' " to " omitted ".
1939 (2 & 3 Geo. 6.) c. 102.	Liability for War Damage (Miscellaneous Provisions) Act 1939.	Sections 4 and 6(*b*).
1940 (3 & 4 Geo. 6.) c. 42.	Law Reform (Miscellaneous Provisions) (Scotland) Act 1940.	In section 4(2), paragraphs (*b*) and (*c*).
1945 (8 & 9 Geo. 6.) c. 16.	Limitation (Enemies and War Prisoners) Act 1945.	In section 2, the words " subsection (1) of section thirteen of the Moneylenders Act 1927 ". In section 4, the words " subsection (1) of section thirteen of the Moneylenders Act 1927".
1948 (11 & 12 Geo. 6.) c. 38.	Companies Act 1948.	Section 201(2)(*c*).
1949 (12 & 13 Geo. 6.) c. 47.	Finance Act 1949.	In section 15, subsections (1) to (3) and (6) to (8A).
1952 (15 & 16 Geo. 6 & 1 Eliz. 2.) c. 44.	Customs and Excise Act 1952.	In section 313(1) the words " or section fifteen of the Finance Act 1949 ".
1956 (4 & 5 Eliz. 2.) c. 68.	Restrictive Trade Practices Act 1956.	Section 26(4) from "and for the reference to a hire-purchase agreement' 'onwards. Section 26(5).
1960 (8 & 9 Eliz. 2.) c. 24.	Pawnbrokers Act 1960.	The whole Act.
1961 (9 & 10 Eliz. 2.) c. 36.	Finance Act 1961.	Section 11(1) from " or section 15 of the Finance Act 1949 " onwards.
1964 c. 42.	Administration of Justice Act 1964.	Section 9(3)(*b*).
1964 c. 53.	Hire-Purchase Act 1964.	The whole Act, except Part III and section 37.
1964 c. 60.	Emergency Laws (Re-enactment and Repeals) Act 1964.	Section 1(4).
1964 c. 71.	Trading Stamps Act 1964.	In section 10(1) the definition of " purchase ".
1965 c. 66.	Hire-Purchase Act 1965.	The whole Act.
1965 c. 67.	Hire-Purchase (Scotland) Act 1965.	The whole Act.
1966 c. 42.	Local Government Act 1966.	In Schedule 3, Part II, the entries relating to section 37 of the Pawnbrokers Act 1872. and section 1(1) of the Moneylenders Act 1927.

Chapter	Short Title	Extent of Repeal
1966 c. 51.	Local Government (Scotland) Act 1966.	In Schedule 4, Part II, the entries relating to section 37 of the Pawnbrokers Act 1872 and section 1(1) of the Moneylenders Act 1927.
1967 c. 42.	Advertisements (Hire-Purchase) Act 1967.	The whole Act.
1967 c. 81.	Companies Act 1967.	Sections 123 to 125.
1968 c. 60.	Theft Act 1968.	In Schedule 2, Part III, the entry relating to the Pawnbrokers Act 1872.
1969 c. 19.	Decimal Currency Act 1969.	In Schedule 2, paragraph 2.
1969 c. 48.	Post Office Act 1969.	In Schedule 4, paragraph 31.
1971 c. 23.	Courts Act 1971.	In Schedule 9, Part I, the entries relating to the Pawnbrokers Act 1872 and the Moneylenders Act 1927.
1972 c. 70.	Local Government Act 1972.	Section 213(1)(*a*) and (*b*) and (3).
1973 c. 65.	Local Government (Scotland) Act 1973.	In Schedule 27, paragraph 96. In Schedule 29, the entry relating to the Finance Act 1949.

PART II
NORTHERN IRELAND

Chapter	Short Title	Extent of Repeal
1842 (5 & 6 Vict.) c. 75.	Charitable Pawn Offices (Ireland) Act 1842.	The whole Act.
1933 c. 23 (N.I.).	Money lenders Act (Northern Ireland) 1933.	The whole Act.
1939 c. 36 (N.I.).	Liability for War Damage (Miscellaneous Provisions) Act (Northern Ireland) 1939.	In section 5(1) the definition of " hire-purchase agreement ".
1949 c. 2 (N.I.).	Agriculture Act (Northern Ireland) 1949.	Section 7(2).
1954 c. 30 (N.I.).	Pawnbrokers Act (Northern Ireland) 1954.	The whole Act.
1957 c. 19 (N.I.).	Betting and Lotteries Act (Northern Ireland) 1957	Section 3(1)(*j*).
1960 c. 22 (N.I.).	Companies Act (Northern Ireland) 1960.	Section 192(3)(*c*).
1965 c. 6 (N.I.).	Trading Stamps Act (Northern Ireland) 1965.	In section 9 the definition of " purchase ".
1966 c. 42 (N.I.).	Hire-Purchase Act (Northern Ireland) 1966.	The whole Act except Part VI and section 68.
1967 c. 29 (N.I.).	Increase of Fines Act (Northern Ireland) 1967.	In Part I of the Schedule the entries relating to the Moneylenders Act (Northern Ireland) 1933.

SCH. 5

Chapter	Short Title	Extent of Repeal
1968 c. 28 (N.I.).	Criminal Justice (Miscellaneous Provisions) Act (Northern Ireland) 1968.	In Schedule 2 the entry relating to the Moneylenders Act (Northern Ireland) 1933.
1969 c. 16 (N.I.).	Theft Act (Northern Ireland) 1969.	In Schedule 2 the entry relating to the Pawnbrokers Act (Northern Ireland) 1954.
1969 c. 24 (N.I.).	Industrial and Provident Societies Act (Northern Ireland) 1969.	Section 96.
1969 c. 27 (N.I.).	Moneylenders (Amendment) Act (Northern Ireland) 1969.	The whole Act.
1969 c. 30 (N.I.).	Judgments (Enforcement) Act (Northern Ireland) 1969.	In Schedule 4 the amendments of the Hire-Purchase Act (Northern Ireland) 1966.
1971 c. 13 (N.I.).	Licensing Act (Northern Ireland) 1971.	Section 2(5)(*b*).
1972 c. 11 (N.I.).	Miscellaneous Transferred Excise Duties Act (Northern Ireland) 1972.	Parts VI and VII. In Schedule 4 the entry relating to the Pawnbrokers Act (Northern Ireland) 1954.

PRODUCED IN ENGLAND BY COMMERCIAL COLOUR PRESS LONDON
FOR BERNARD M THIMONT
Controller of Her Majesty's Stationery Office and Queen's Printer of Acts of Parliament

CORRECTIONS

Errors appear in the first impression (October 1974) of this Act and the following corrections have been incorporated into this reprint.

Page 115, Schedule 1, Section 1,

> *for* " 9(1) " *read* " 39(1) " and
> *for* " 9(2) " *read* " 39(2) "

Dd.290944 K20 2/78 CCP